It's another Quality Book from CGP

*This book has been carefully written for
children working towards a Level 5.*

It matches the Attainment Targets perfectly.

*There's lots of stuff to learn if you want to get a Level 5.
Happily this CGP book explains all the important information
as clearly and simply as possible.*

*It's also got some daft bits in to try and make the whole experience
at least vaguely entertaining for you.*

What CGP is all about

*Our sole aim here at CGP is to produce the highest quality books
— carefully written, immaculately presented and
dangerously close to being funny.*

*Then we work our socks off to get them out to you
— at the cheapest possible prices.*

Contents

SECTION FOUR — UNDERSTANDING SHAPE

SECTION FIVE — MEASURING

SECTION SIX — HANDLING DATA

SECTION SEVEN — USING AND APPLYING MATHEMATICS

Published by CGP

Editors:
Charlotte Burrows, Katherine Craig, Charley Darbishire, Sarah Hilton, Sharon Keeley,
Rob MacDonald, Andy Park, Julie Wakeling, Sarah Williams.

Contributor:
Andrew Ross

Key Stage Two Consultant:
John Cullen

ISBN: 978 1 84762 196 2

With thanks to Ali Palin, Isabelle Darbishire and Tina Ramsden for the proofreading.

Groovy website: www.cgpbooks.co.uk

With thanks to Jan Greenway for the copyright research.
Thumb illustration used throughout the book © iStockphoto.com.

Printed by Elanders Ltd, Newcastle upon Tyne.
Jolly bits of clipart from CorelDRAW®

Based on the classic CGP style created by Richard Parsons.

About the Book

This Book has All the Tricky Topics for Level 5

You've got a good chance of getting a <u>Level 5</u> if you can do <u>all the maths</u> in this book.

There are a couple of pages on each topic.

One page <u>explains</u> the maths.

The other page has <u>worked examples</u>.

These show you how to answer questions.

> This book covers all the <u>Attainment Targets</u> for Level 5. They say what maths children working at Level 5 can usually do.

There are Practice Questions for Each Section

At the end of each section are <u>practice questions</u>.

You can see what you know and what you don't know.

There's a <u>matching Level 5 Question Book</u>.

It's got questions on all the topics.

It also has some practice tests too.

> I love to practise.
> I love to practise.

There are Learning Objectives on All Pages

Learning Objectives say <u>what you need to know</u>.

Use the <u>tick circles</u> to show how well you understand the maths.

Use a pencil. You can <u>tick other circles</u> as you get better.

> I can win gold at the Olympics.

> Tick here if you can do some of the Learning Objective.

> If you're struggling, tick here.

> Tick this circle if you can do the Learning Objective really well.

Learning Objective:

"I can use the memory of a calculator, bracket keys and the square root button."

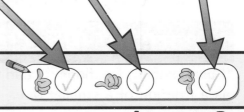

Fractions

Simplifying — Divide the Top and Bottom

Simplifying a fraction means making an equivalent fraction that has the smallest numerator and denominator possible.

You just divide the numerator (top number) and denominator (bottom number) by the biggest number that goes into both.

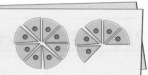

$$\frac{6}{12} \xrightarrow{\div 6} \frac{1}{2} \xleftarrow{\div 6}$$

Or... do it in stages.

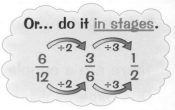

$$\frac{6}{12} \xrightarrow{\div 2} \frac{3}{6} \xrightarrow{\div 3} \frac{1}{2}$$

Some Fractions are Bigger Than 1

You can use improper fractions or mixed numbers to write fractions bigger than 1.

EXAMPLE: Jacob buys some cakes. He cuts each cake into 8 equal slices. After a party he has 13 slices left. Write the number of cakes left as a mixed number.

 1 cake = 8 slices. So the number of cakes left as a fraction will have a denominator of 8.

This is an improper fraction.

There are 13 slices left. So the number of cakes left is $\frac{13}{8}$.

Now write $\frac{13}{8}$ as a mixed number: $\frac{13}{8} = \frac{8}{8} + \frac{5}{8} = 1\frac{5}{8}$.

This is one whole.

You Can Put Fractions in Order

For fractions with the **SAME** denominator ⟶ compare numerators.

For fractions with **DIFFERENT** denominators ⟶ find equivalent fractions with the same denominator (then compare numerators).

EXAMPLE: Order these fractions from smallest to largest: $\frac{1}{3}$, $\frac{3}{4}$ and $\frac{3}{12}$.

Step 1: Find a common denominator. You need a number that's a multiple of all your denominators. 3, 4 and 12 all have 12 as a multiple, so use that.

Step 2: Make equivalent fractions that have your common denominator. ($\frac{3}{12}$ already has 12 as its denominator.)

$$\frac{1}{3} \xrightarrow{\times 4} \frac{4}{12} \qquad \frac{3}{4} \xrightarrow{\times 3} \frac{9}{12}$$

Step 3: Write out all the fractions and compare numerators.

$$\frac{4}{12}, \frac{9}{12}, \frac{3}{12} \longrightarrow$$ So from smallest to largest, the order is $\frac{3}{12}, \frac{4}{12}, \frac{9}{12}$

Now change the fractions back to the ones in the question.

 $$\boxed{\frac{3}{12}, \frac{1}{3}, \frac{3}{4}}$$

Learning Objective:

"I can simplify fractions. I can write a larger whole number as a fraction of a smaller one. I can put fractions in order."

Fractions

Question 1

Which two numbers in this list have the same value? $\frac{10}{16}$ $\frac{2}{5}$ $\frac{3}{4}$ $\frac{5}{8}$ $\frac{9}{15}$ $\frac{8}{12}$

1 <u>Simplify</u> any fractions you can.

2 Write out the <u>whole list</u> again, but include your <u>simplified</u> fractions too.

3 Choose the fractions from the list with the <u>same value</u>.

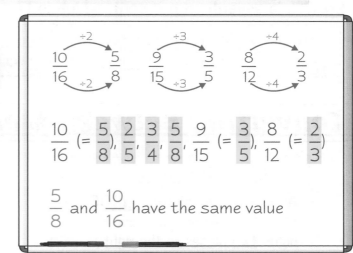

$$\frac{10}{16} \xrightarrow{\div 2} \frac{5}{8} \qquad \frac{9}{15} \xrightarrow{\div 3} \frac{3}{5} \qquad \frac{8}{12} \xrightarrow{\div 4} \frac{2}{3}$$

$$\frac{10}{16}\left(=\frac{5}{8}\right), \frac{2}{5}, \frac{3}{4}, \frac{5}{8}, \frac{9}{15}\left(=\frac{3}{5}\right), \frac{8}{12}\left(=\frac{2}{3}\right)$$

$$\frac{5}{8} \text{ and } \frac{10}{16} \text{ have the same value}$$

Question 2

Put these fractions in order of size, starting with the smallest.

$$\frac{1}{2} \qquad \frac{2}{3} \qquad \frac{5}{9}$$

1 Decide on a <u>common denominator</u>.

2 Make <u>equivalent fractions</u> that all have **18** as the denominator.

3 Arrange these fractions <u>in order</u>, from smallest to biggest.

4 Change these back to the fractions in the <u>question</u>.

2, 3 and 9 all have 18 as a multiple.
So use 18 as a common denominator.

$$\frac{1}{2} \xrightarrow{\times 9} = \frac{9}{18} \qquad \frac{2}{3} \xrightarrow{\times 6} = \frac{12}{18} \qquad \frac{5}{9} \xrightarrow{\times 2} = \frac{10}{18}$$

In order of size: $\frac{9}{18} \quad \frac{10}{18} \quad \frac{12}{18}$

$$\frac{1}{2} \qquad \frac{5}{9} \qquad \frac{2}{3}$$

Equivalent fractions are really useful...

Simplifying fractions is good, because all the numbers end up smaller and easier to use. Remember, you have to divide both the numerator and denominator by the same number.

Percentages

"Per Cent" Means "Out of 100"

% is a short way of writing <u>per cent</u>, and it just means "<u>out of 100</u>".
So 17% is seventeen per cent, which is 17 out of 100.

> You can write any percentage as a <u>fraction</u>. Write the
> <u>percentage</u> as the <u>numerator</u> and <u>100</u> as the <u>denominator</u>.

EXAMPLE:

$17\% = \frac{17}{100}$

Converting Between % and Decimals — Easy

% to Decimals

All you do is <u>divide by 100</u>.
(That just means you move the
digits <u>two places to the right</u>.)

Decimals to %

All you do is <u>multiply by 100</u>.
(That just means you move the
digits <u>two places to the left</u>.)

EXAMPLES: a) Write **47%** as a decimal.
                b) Write **0.62** as a percentage.

<u>ANSWERS</u>:   a) 47% = 47 ÷ 100 = <u>0.47</u>
                b) 0.62 × 100% = <u>62%</u>

Fractions to Percentages — Slightly Trickier

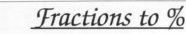

Fractions to %

1)   You need to <u>convert</u> the fraction to a <u>decimal</u> first.
   (Divide the <u>numerator</u> by the <u>denominator</u>. Use a <u>calculator</u> if the fraction is tricky.)

2)   Then turn it into a <u>percentage</u> like before.

EXAMPLE: Write $\frac{3}{10}$ as a percentage. | 3 ÷ 10 = 0.3 then 0.3 × 100% = <u>30%</u>

Write an Amount as a Percentage of Another

EXAMPLE: Gerald needs 1000 frogs to make frog soup.
He collects 550. What percentage of his total is this?

He's got <u>550 out of the 1000</u> he needs.

1)   Write this as a <u>fraction</u>: $\frac{550}{1000}$

2)   Convert the fraction into a <u>percentage</u>: $\frac{550}{1000} = 0.55$

                                           0.55 × 100% = <u>55%</u>

Learning Objective:

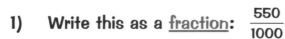

"I can convert between fractions, decimals and percentages.
I can write an amount as a percentage of another."

Percentages

Question 1

Complete this table of decimals, fractions and percentages.

Give your fractions in their simplest form.

Fraction	Decimal	Percentage
$\frac{13}{20}$		
		59%
	0.65	

1 To convert $\frac{13}{20}$ to a decimal, <u>divide</u> the numerator by the denominator.
<u>Multiply this by 100</u> to convert to a percentage.

2 To convert 59% to a decimal, <u>divide by 100</u>.
Convert to a fraction by writing the <u>percentage</u> as the <u>numerator</u> and <u>100</u> as the <u>denominator</u>.

3 To convert 0.65 to a percentage, <u>multiply by 100</u>.
Convert to a fraction by writing the <u>percentage</u> as the <u>numerator</u> and <u>100</u> as the <u>denominator</u>.
Remember to <u>simplify</u> the fraction.

Row 1: $13 \div 20 = 0.65$
$0.65 \times 100\% = 65\%$

Row 2: $59 \div 100 = 0.59$
$59\% = \frac{59}{100}$

Row 3: $0.65 \times 100\% = 65\%$
$65\% = \frac{65}{100} = \frac{13}{20}$

Question 2

Konnie is saving up to buy a new bicycle that costs £80. So far she has saved £35.

a)   What percentage of the total cost of the bicycle has Konnie saved so far?

b)   Ed wants to buy a bicycle costing £120. He has saved £48 so far. Who, out of Konnie and Ed, has saved the bigger percentage of the cost of their bicycle?

a) **1** First write '35 out of 80' as a <u>fraction</u>.

2 Then convert this to a <u>percentage</u> by dividing...
...and then <u>multiplying by 100</u>.

b) **1** Write 48 as a <u>percentage</u> of 120.

2 <u>Compare</u> this to your part a) answer.

a) $\frac{35}{80}$
$35 \div 80 = 0.4375$
$0.4375 \times 100\% = 43.75\%$

b) $\frac{48}{120} = 48 \div 120 = 0.4$
This is $0.4 \times 100\% = 40\%$.
Konnie has saved the bigger %

Percentages — not as difficult as they sound...

If you remember that a <u>fraction</u> shows <u>division</u>, converting a fraction to a decimal is easy.
And to convert between decimals and percentages just multiply or divide by 100.

Numbers and Number Lines

Adding and Subtracting Negative Numbers

Number lines are really useful for problems that have <u>negative numbers</u> in.

They're going to get it wrong. I just know it.

Don't be so negative.

EXAMPLE: What is -7 + 6?

Start at -7

Count on 6 places

-8 -7 -6 -5 -4 -3 -2 -1 0

The answer is **-1**

EXAMPLE: Work out -4 – 13.

Count back 10 places, then 3 places

Start at -4

-20   -17   -14   -10   -4   0

The answer is **-17**

Put Negative Numbers in the Right Order

EXAMPLE: The temperatures in four towns are 7 °C, –3 °C, –9 °C and 2 °C. Put these temperatures in order, starting with the coldest.

Start by drawing a <u>number line</u> and marking on the temperatures.

Remember... <u>negative</u> numbers go to the <u>left</u> of zero.

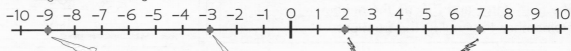

–10 –9 –8 –7 –6 –5 –4 –3 –2 –1 0 1 2 3 4 5 6 7 8 9 10

The <u>coldest</u> is –9 °C...   ...then –3 °C...   ...then 2 °C... ...meaning 7 °C is the <u>warmest</u>.
So the correct order is –9 °C, –3 °C, 2 °C, 7 °C.

Working Out Differences

EXAMPLE: The temperature in Neil's freezer was -9 °C. Neil filled his freezer with shoes. The temperature rose to 2 °C. What was the <u>rise</u> in temperature?

Do a quick sketch of the number line. Mark the two temperatures on it then <u>count how many degrees</u> there are between them.

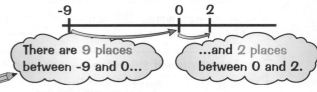

-9   0 2

There are 9 places between -9 and 0...

...and 2 places between 0 and 2.

It's often easiest to count the places <u>to zero</u>, then the number of places <u>after zero</u> and then add them together... 9 + 2 = <u>11 °C</u>.

EXAMPLE:

The temperature in Icetown is -46 °C.
The temperature in Froston is -12 °C.
Find the difference between these temperatures.

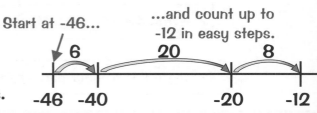

Start at -46...

...and count up to -12 in easy steps.

6   20   8

-46 -40   -20   -12

So the difference is 6 + 20 + 8 = <u>34 °C</u>.

Learning Objective:

"I can find the difference between positive and negative integers."

Numbers and Number Lines

Question 1

Sandy makes a sequence of numbers.
She starts with 40, and subtracts 15 to make each new term.   40, 25, 10, ... , ...
Write the **next two numbers** in the sequence.

1 Draw a number line. Mark on the terms of the sequence you're given.

2 Subtract 15 to find each new term.

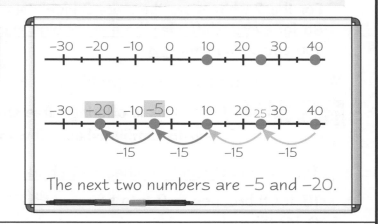

The next two numbers are −5 and −20.

Question 2

a)   Between midday and midnight, the temperature in Grizebeck fell from −3 °C to −45 °C.
     Find the difference between the midday temperature and the midnight temperature.

b)   In Swayton, the temperature is 22 °C. The temperature then falls by 37 degrees.
     Find the new temperature in Swayton.

a) **1** Draw a number line. Show the numbers from the question.

2 The difference between the temperatures is the number of degrees between them. Count on from −45 in easy steps.

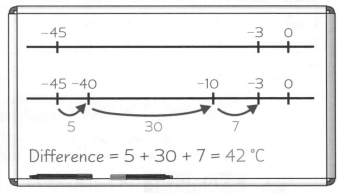

Difference = 5 + 30 + 7 = 42 °C

b) **1** Show the information on a number line.

2 Start at 22, then count 37 degrees back in easy steps.

3 Don't forget the minus sign in the answer.

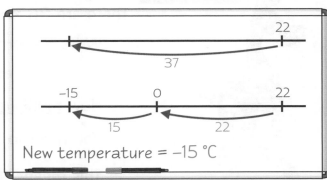

New temperature = −15 °C

Finding a difference means subtracting...

It's always good in maths to draw a diagram whenever you can, and number lines are a very
useful kind of diagram. They're really handy when you're using negative numbers.

Proportion and Ratio

Ratios Compare One Part to Another Part

Look at this pattern:

For the 2 white stars there are 6 blue stars.
So <u>for every white star there are 3 blue stars</u>. The <u>ratio</u> is <u>1 white</u> to <u>3 blue</u>.
You could also write <u>1:3</u>.

You can use ratios to solve problems.

EXAMPLE: Crazy Jack is offering 1 free shark with every 6 toothbrushes bought.
I buy 18 toothbrushes. How many free sharks will I get?

The ratio is <u>6 toothbrushes</u> to <u>1 shark</u>.

18 toothbrushes is <u>3 lots</u> of
<u>6 toothbrushes.</u>

So I get <u>3 lots</u> of <u>1 free shark</u>.
$3 \times 1 = $ <u>3 free sharks</u>.

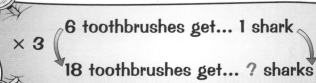

6 toothbrushes get... 1 shark
$\times 3$
18 toothbrushes get... ? sharks
$\times 3$

Proportions Compare a Part to the Whole Thing

Look again at the star pattern at the top of the page. You can describe it another way.
<u>In every 4 stars there are 3 blue stars and 1 white star</u>.

The <u>proportion</u> of blue stars is <u>3 in every 4</u>. The <u>proportion</u> of white stars is <u>1 in every 4</u>.

Proportions are really another way of writing fractions.
The proportion "1 in every 4" is the same as the fraction $\frac{1}{4}$.

EXAMPLE: In my herd of zebras, 2 in every 9 zebras are <u>orange</u>.
There are 36 zebras in my herd. How many are orange?

Write the proportion as a <u>fraction</u>...

<u>2</u> in every <u>9</u> is the same as $\frac{2}{9}$.

Now <u>multiply</u> your fraction by the <u>total</u> number of zebras.

You need to find $36 \times \frac{2}{9} \implies 36 \div 9 = 4$, and $4 \times 2 = 8$.

This means there are <u>8 orange zebras</u>.

Learning Objective:

"I can solve problems using ratio and proportion."

Proportion and Ratio

Question 1

Grapes cost 90p for 360 grams.

a)   How many grams of grapes could I buy for £2.70?

b)   What is the cost of 900 grams of grapes?

a)

1 Write down the ratio you <u>know</u>.

2 Write down the ratio you need to <u>find out</u>.

3 The left-hand side of your first ratio has been <u>multiplied by 3</u>. So multiply the <u>right-hand side</u> by 3 too.

b)

1 Write down the ratio you <u>know</u>.

2 Write down the ratio you need to <u>find out</u>.

3 Work out what the <u>right-hand</u> side has been multiplied by — this is **900 ÷ 360 = <u>2.5</u>**. So multiply the <u>left-hand</u> side by 2.5 too.

90p	for	360 grams
↓		↓
£2.70	for	??? grams

90p	for	360 grams
↓ × 3		↓ × 3
£2.70	for	1080 grams

90p	for	360 grams
↓		↓
???	for	900 grams

90p	for	360 grams
↓ × 2.5		↓ × 2.5
£2.25	for	900 grams

Question 2

A red box and a green box have a total mass of 360 grams.
The mass of the red box is three times as much as the mass of the green box.
What is the mass of each box?

1 Write a <u>ratio</u> of the two masses.

2 Calculate what <u>proportion</u> each box is of the total mass.

3 <u>Multiply</u> these fractions by the total mass to find the mass of each box.

Mass of red box : mass of green box is 3 : 1

3 + 1 = 4 parts altogether.
So the red box is $\frac{3}{4}$ of the total mass
and the green box is $\frac{1}{4}$ of the total mass.

For red box, $\frac{3}{4}$ of $360 = \frac{3}{4} \times 360 = 270$ g

For green box, $\frac{1}{4}$ of $360 = \frac{1}{4} \times 360 = 90$ g

Always multiply or divide both sides of a ratio...

You have to think carefully when you write proportions. In Question 2, the ratio is <u>**3 : 1**</u> but the proportions are <u>quarters</u> (not thirds) because there are 4 parts altogether.

Practice Questions

1   Simplify these fractions as much as possible:

 a) $\dfrac{15}{10}$ b) $\dfrac{12}{18}$ c) $\dfrac{36}{48}$

2   Convert these improper fractions to mixed numbers.

 a) $\dfrac{5}{2}$ b) $\dfrac{11}{3}$ c) $\dfrac{25}{6}$

3   Kevin buys some apples for an apple crumble. He cuts them all into quarters.
    After making the apple crumble, Kevin has 19 apple quarters left over.

    Write the number of apples Kevin has left as a mixed number.

4   Write these fractions in order of size. Start with the smallest.

 $\dfrac{5}{6}$ $\dfrac{3}{4}$ $\dfrac{2}{3}$

5   Natalya takes three tests at school.
    Her results are shown in this table.

    Natalya's parents want to know
    each of her three scores as:
    - a percentage,
    - a decimal,
    - a fraction.

	Percentage	Decimal	Fraction
English	85%		
Maths			$\dfrac{47}{50}$
Science		0.44	

   Copy and complete the table to show the three scores in the three different forms.
   Give your fractions in their simplest form.

6   This table shows the temperatures in five people's fridges.

    Write the five temperatures in order, starting with the lowest.

Areti	−1 °C
Daniel	−9 °C
Eva	6 °C
Aishah	−5 °C
Costas	1 °C

Practice Questions

7   The table below shows the temperatures at midday and midnight in four different towns.

Town	Temperature at midday (°C)	Temperature at midnight (°C)	Temperature difference (°C)
Normalsville	22	4	18
Heaton	39	26	
Nippiham	4	−7	
Chillbeck	−6	−14	

Copy and complete the table to find the difference between the midday temperature and the midnight temperature for each town.

The first one has been done for you.

8   Charlotte's younger sister has a set of wooden shapes.
She picks the shapes shown below out of the set.

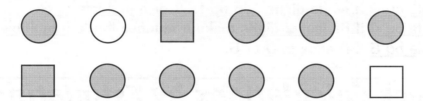

a)   What is the ratio of circles to squares?

b)   What is the ratio of white shapes to grey shapes?

c)   What proportion of the shapes are grey circles?

9   One in every three biscuits in a biscuit tin is a ginger nut.
There are 33 biscuits in the tin.

How many ginger nuts are there in the tin?

10   In the zoo, two out of every five penguins have a black beak.
There are eight penguins with black beaks.

How many penguins **do not** have black beaks?

Checking Calculations

Use Inverses to Check Calculations

One way to check an answer is to do the <u>inverse</u> calculation.
You should get back to the number <u>you started with</u>.

> 'Inverse' just means 'opposite'.

Remember:

> ADDITION and SUBTRACTION are inverses.

EXAMPLE: What is 6.3 − 4.5?
Step 1) <u>DO IT:</u> 6.3 − 4.5 = 1.8
Step 2) <u>CHECK IT:</u> 1.8 + 4.5 = 6.3 ✓

EXAMPLE: What is 72 ÷ 6?
Step 1) <u>DO IT:</u> 72 ÷ 6 = 12
Step 2) <u>CHECK IT:</u> 12 × 6 = 72 ✓

> MULTIPLICATION and DIVISION are inverses.

Divisibility

You can check <u>multiplications</u> by doing a test of <u>divisibility</u>.

EXAMPLE: If you work out <u>247 × 9</u>, the answer must be <u>divisible by 9</u>.
A number is divisible by 9 if all its digits <u>add up to 9</u> or a <u>multiple of 9</u>.

Here are some more tests of divisibility:
A number is <u>divisible by 3</u> if all its digits <u>add up to 3</u> or a <u>multiple of 3</u>.
A number is <u>divisible by 4</u> if its <u>last 2 digits</u> make a number that's <u>a multiple of 4</u>, e.g. 308
A number is <u>divisible by 5</u> if it ends in <u>0</u> or <u>5</u>.

You Can Check Calculations by Estimating

When you estimate things,
use a bendy equals sign like this: ≈ It means "is <u>approximately</u> equal to".

> That's "<u>about</u>" to the rest of us.

> So 21 × 32 ≈ 600 means "21 × 32 <u>is about</u> 600."

EXAMPLE: Bessie flies 9.81 km every second.
How far does she travel in 8.6 seconds?

The <u>exact</u> distance she travels is 9.81 × 8.6 km.
Here is the <u>approximation</u>:

> 9.81 × 8.6 ≈ 10 × 9 = <u>90 km</u>

For this estimate, it's easiest to round to the nearest whole number.

So you know the answer is going to be <u>somewhere near</u> 90.

The answer should be a bit <u>less than 90</u>,
because you rounded both numbers up.
If your answer <u>isn't</u> a bit less than 90, <u>try again</u>.

Learning Objective:

"I can estimate and check the result of a calculation."

Checking Calculations

Question 1

Michael works out 279 × 4 three times and gets three different answers: **1114**, **1116** and **1118**.
a)   Which one of Michael's answers could be correct?
b)   Write down a calculation that Michael could use to check this answer.

a

The answer to **279 × 4** must be divisible by 4.
A number is divisible by 4 if its <u>last 2 digits</u>
make a number that's <u>a multiple of 4</u>.
Check the <u>last 2 digits</u> of all three 'answers'
and write down which one could be correct.

b

From part a) you know that the calculation
is 279 × 4 = 1116. Work out the <u>inverse
calculation</u>, which is a division.

a)   11<u>14</u> — 14 isn't a multiple of 4 so
                        this can't be right.

       11<u>16</u> — 16 <u>is</u> a multiple of 4 so
                        this could be right.

       11<u>18</u> — 18 isn't a multiple of 4 so
                        this can't be right.

       279 × 4 = 1116 could be
       correct.

b)   1116 ÷ 4

Question 2

Estimate the value of 8.2 × 3.3.
Will the exact value be bigger or smaller than your estimate?

1

<u>Round</u> each of the numbers to
the nearest whole number.

2

Use the rounded numbers to
write an <u>approximate calculation</u>.
Work out the <u>answer</u> to your
approximate calculation.

3

Both numbers were <u>rounded down</u>, so
the estimate is <u>too small</u>. The exact
value will be <u>bigger</u> than the estimate.

8.2 rounds down to 8.
3.3 rounds down to 3.

8.2 × 3.3 ≈ 8 × 3
         8 × 3 = 24

The exact value will be bigger.

It's a good idea to check your calculations...

Estimating an answer helps you to check your calculation. Round the numbers and write
an approximate calculation. Then work this out and check it against the exact calculation.

Factors and Multiples

A Number is Divisible by its Factors

The factors of a number are whole numbers that divide exactly into that number. (Two factors will multiply together to give the number.)

I shall divide and conquer...

A number is divisible by all its factors.
For example, 9 is divisible by its factors 1, 3 and 9.
9 is a multiple of 1, 3 and 9.

PRIME Numbers Only Have Two Factors

A prime number is a number that has exactly TWO FACTORS: 1 and itself.

EXAMPLE: The only numbers that multiply to give 23 are 1 and 23.
23 only divides exactly by 1 and 23, so it's prime.

1	(2)	(3)	4	(5)	6	(7)	8	9	10
(11)	12	(13)	14	15	16	(17)	18	(19)	20
21	22	(23)	24	25	26	27	28	(29)	30
(31)	32	33	34	35	36	(37)	38	39	40
(41)	42	(43)	44	45	46	(47)	48	49	50
51	52	(53)	54	55	56	57	58	(59)	60
(61)	62	63	64	65	66	(67)	68	69	70
(71)	72	(73)	74	75	76	77	78	(79)	80
81	82	(83)	84	85	86	87	88	(89)	90
91	92	93	94	95	96	(97)	98	99	100

All the circled numbers in this grid are prime numbers.

1) 1 is NOT a prime number — it doesn't have exactly 2 factors.
2) All prime numbers end in 1, 3, 7 or 9. 2 and 5 are the exceptions.
3) 2 is the only even prime.

BUT not all numbers ending in 1, 3, 7 or 9 are prime.

Finding Prime Factors

Whole numbers that aren't prime are made up of prime numbers multiplied together. These prime numbers are called prime factors.

All apart from 1.

EXAMPLE: Which prime numbers multiply together to make 56?

(1) Write down any factor pair of 56. → 56 = 7 × 8

(2) 7 is a prime number. It is a prime factor of 56. 8 isn't prime, so split it up into a factor pair. → 56 = 7 × 2 × 4 (✓prime ✓prime)

(3) 2 is prime. 4 isn't, so split 4 into 2 × 2. → 56 = 7 × 2 × 2 × 2 (✓prime ✓prime)

Now all the factors are prime.

Learning Objective:

"I can tell you all the prime numbers up to 100 and find the prime factors of other numbers."

Factors and Multiples

Question 1

Paul is thinking of a whole number. Alice asks him the four questions below to work it out.

1. Is it under 85? No
2. Is it below 95? Yes
3. Is it a multiple of two? No
4. Is it a prime number? Yes

What number is Paul thinking of?

1 From question 1 you know that the number is <u>85 or greater</u>.

2 From question 2, it's <u>less than 95</u>.

3 The number isn't a multiple of two, so it must be an <u>odd number</u>.

4 The number is a <u>prime number</u> that is greater than 84 and less than 95.

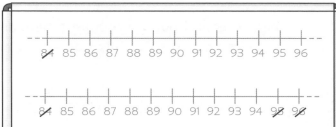

Paul's number is greater than 84 and less than 95, and is an odd number. So it could be 85, 87, 89, 91 or 93.

The only prime number greater than 84 and less than 95 is 89.

Question 2

Fill in the four prime numbers which multiply to make 60. ☐ × ☐ × ☐ × ☐ = 60

1 Write down a <u>factor pair</u> of 60. (There's more than one you could pick.)

2 10 and 6 aren't prime numbers so split <u>them</u> up into factor pairs, until you get <u>just prime numbers</u>. <u>2</u>, <u>3</u> and <u>5</u> are prime numbers.

3 Write down the <u>correct answer</u>.

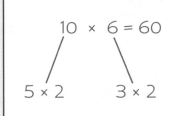

10 × 6 = 60

5 × 2   3 × 2

So 5 × 2 × 3 × 2 = 60

5 × 2 × 3 × 2 = 60

(You could also start with <u>5 × 12</u> or <u>4 × 15</u> or <u>3 × 20</u> or <u>2 × 30</u>.)

However you start off, you'll end up with the <u>same final answer</u>.

Prime numbers only divide by themselves and 1...

Make sure you know the rules to help you spot prime numbers below 100 — they're all odd (except 2) and they all end in 1, 3, 7 or 9 (except for 5 and 2).

Square Numbers

Square Numbers

When you multiply a whole number by itself, you get a <u>SQUARE NUMBER</u>.
Here are the first few square numbers:

1	4	9	16	25	36	49	64	81	100	121	144...
(1×1)	(2×2)	(3×3)	(4×4)	(5×5)	(6×6)	(7×7)	(8×8)	(9×9)	(10×10)	(11×11)	(12×12)...

They're called <u>square numbers</u> because
they are the areas in this pattern of squares.

You can say this
as "3 squared".

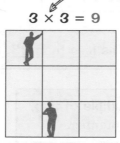

$3 \times 3 = 9$

$4 \times 4 = 16$

$1 \times 1 = 1$

$2 \times 2 = 4$

There's a quick way to write them.
You write 5×5 as 5^2 or "<u>five squared</u>".

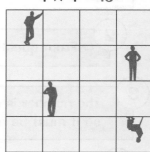

Work hard to get ahead.

But I've already got a head.

EXAMPLES:
a) $7^2 = 7$ squared $= 7 \times 7 = 49$.
b) $12^2 = 12$ squared $= 12 \times 12 = 144$.

You can easily work out numbers like 30^2 and 40^2 too.

EXAMPLE: What is 40^2?

$$40^2 = 40 \times 40$$
$$= 4 \times 10 \times 4 \times 10$$
$$= 4 \times 4 \times 10 \times 10$$
$$= \underline{1600}$$

BE CAREFUL!
It's <u>NOT</u> $4^2 \times 10$

Another Example

Find two different square numbers that add to 50.

Write down square numbers up to 50: 1 4 9 16 25 36 49

It's easy to see that to make 50, you just need to add 1 to 49.

$$1 + 49 = 50$$

Learning Objective:

"I can say the squares of numbers to 12×12
and work out the squares of multiples of 10."

Square Numbers

Question 1

What is the largest square number that is less than 81?

1 Work out which number multiplied by itself gives 81.

2 Since $9 \times 9 = 81$, you need to find 8×8. (8 is the next whole number under 9 so it will produce the next largest square number.)

3 Use your calculation to answer the question.

$9 \times 9 = 81$

$8 \times 8 = 64$

The largest square number less than 81 is 64.

Question 2

What is fifty squared?

1 Write 50^2 as a multiplication.

2 Write both 50s as multiples of 10.

3 Rearrange the multiplication with the tens at the end.

4 Multiply the units together and then the tens.

5 Work out the answer.

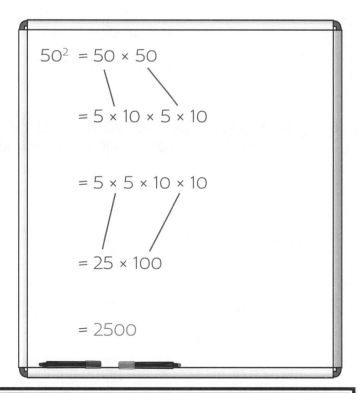

$50^2 = 50 \times 50$

$= 5 \times 10 \times 5 \times 10$

$= 5 \times 5 \times 10 \times 10$

$= 25 \times 100$

$= 2500$

A number multiplied by itself is square...

If you know your times tables, you won't have any problem working out square numbers. All they are is 1×1, 2×2, 3×3,... But make sure you do 20^2, 30^2 and so on properly.

Practice Questions

1   Ellen works out that 584 ÷ 4 = 146.

    Check Ellen's answer by doing an inverse calculation. Is she right or wrong?

2   Tom writes a sequence of numbers that increases by 15 each time: 30, 45, 60, 75, 90 ...
    The sequence continues.

    a)   Will the number 224 be in the sequence?

    b)   Explain your answer.

3   Estimate the value of eighteen point two multiplied by eleven point four.

4   A hotel has 42 floors. There are 27 rooms on each floor.

    Which of the calculations below is the best way to estimate
    how many rooms the hotel has altogether?

                    A   50 × 20 = 1000

                    B   40 × 30 = 1200

                    C   40 × 20 = 800

                    D   50 × 30 = 1500

5   Jane needs to work out 67.51 ÷ 7.28.
    Which of these options is the best **estimate** of the answer?

            7   8   10   11   12   15

6   Write down all the factors of 36.

7   Yinka collects his scores from seven maths tests.

            15   19   34   43   53   63   70

    Which of his scores are prime numbers?

8   Write down all the prime factors of 48.

SECTION TWO — KNOWING AND USING NUMBER FACTS

Practice Questions

9   Write the three prime numbers which multiply to make 105.

     ☐ × ☐ × ☐ = 105

10   Andy is thinking of a whole number. Derek asks him some questions to work it out.

1. Is it less than 40?   Yes

2. Is it greater than 35?   Yes

3. Is it an even number?   No

4. Is it a prime number?   Yes

What number is Andy thinking of?

11   Tim writes this sequence of square numbers. What is the next number?

25   36   49   64   ☐

12   Abdul thinks of a 3-digit square number. Its second digit is 4.

☐ 4 ☐

What are the missing digits in Abdul's number?

13   Anna is thinking of 2 square numbers. She says, "They total 130".
What 2 numbers could Anna be thinking of?

☐ + ☐ = 130

14   Meryl says, "I have 20^2 marbles". David says, "I have 30^2 marbles".

a)   How many marbles does Meryl have?

b)   How many more marbles does David have than Meryl?

Calculators

"Of" Means "Times"

When you're talking about fractions, "of" just means "times".

So to find $\frac{1}{8}$ of 368, you need to work out $\frac{1}{8} \times 368$.

You Can Find Fractions Using a Calculator...

EXAMPLE:

Jan uses $\frac{5}{8}$ of a 6.8 m piece of string to make a tightrope for Colin the hamster. How much string does she use?

You need to find $\frac{5}{8}$ of 6.8 m. That's $\frac{5}{8} \times 6.8$ m.

To multiply a number by a fraction you <u>DIVIDE BY THE DENOMINATOR</u> and <u>MULTIPLY BY THE NUMERATOR</u>.

It <u>doesn't matter</u> whether you <u>divide first</u> or <u>multiply first</u>. So you could do 6.8 × 5 ÷ 8 instead.

So, press: 6 . 8 ÷ 8 × 5 =

The display should read: 4.25   So 4.25 m of string was used.

Make sure you understand what the calculator display means. "4.25" means <u>4 m and 0.25 m</u>, which is <u>4 m and 25 cm</u>.

Finding Percentages Of Amounts

This is very similar to finding <u>fractions</u> of amounts.

That's because a percentage is just a fraction with <u>100 as the denominator</u>.

EXAMPLE: Find 20% of £85.

This is £85 × $\frac{20}{100}$ ➔ £85 × 20 ÷ 100 = <u>£17</u>

Or if you've got a % button on your calculator, you can just press:

8 5 × 2 0 %

Learning Objective:

"I can use a calculator to solve problems involving decimals, fractions and percentages."

Calculators

Question 1

Bev has 3 kg of flour. She uses seven twelfths of it to make 25 giant Yorkshire Puddings. How much flour is in each Yorkshire Pudding? Give your answer in grams.

1 First you need to work out how much flour she uses <u>in total</u>. To find a fraction of a number you <u>multiply</u>.

2 Do this fraction multiplication on your <u>calculator</u>. Remember — <u>multiply</u> by the numerator, <u>divide</u> by the denominator.

3 So there's 1.75 kg of flour in 25 Yorkshire Puddings. Now you need to find out how much is in <u>each</u>, so <u>divide by 25</u>.

4 The question asks for the answer in <u>grams</u>. Multiply the amount in kg by 1000.

Bev uses $\frac{7}{12}$ of 3 kg = 3 kg × $\frac{7}{12}$

$$3 \times 7 \div 12 =$$
$$1.75$$

$$1 . 7 5 \div 2 5 =$$
$$0.07$$

Remember, this is in kg.

There are 1000 g in a kilogram.
0.07 × 1000 = 70 g

Question 2

Mr Davis asked 5200 children, "Which country would you most like to visit?" 45% of the children said America and 22% said Wales. How many did not say America or Wales?

1 The percentages must all add up to <u>100</u>. So to find the percentage that <u>didn't</u> say America or Wales, <u>subtract</u> these percentages from 100.

2 Now you just need to find <u>33% of 5200 children</u>. Write this as a <u>fraction multiplication</u>.

3 Do this fraction multiplication on your <u>calculator</u>. Remember — <u>divide</u> by the denominator, <u>multiply</u> by the numerator.

100% – 45% – 22% = 33%
So 33% did not say America or Wales.

33% of 5200 = 5200 × $\frac{33}{100}$

$$5 2 0 0 \div 1 0 0 \times 3 3 =$$
$$1716$$

So, 1716 children didn't say America or Wales.

Multiply by the numerator, divide by the denominator...

Make sure you read the display on your calculator correctly. If the answer is a decimal, think about which decimal place means tenths, which means hundredths and so on.

Calculators

A lot of problems need <u>more than one calculation</u> to solve them.

Use the Memory Button in Multi-Step Problems

You often have to use the <u>answer from one step</u> to do the next step.
That's when the memory buttons on your calculator are handy.

> Press **M+** to <u>store</u> a number in the calculator memory.

> Press **MR** to <u>recall</u> a number so you can use it.

Different calculators have different memory buttons.
Check out the buttons on your own calculator, and make sure you know how they work.

EXAMPLE: Divide 76 by 5. Subtract the answer from 50.

1) First work out 76 ÷ 5: 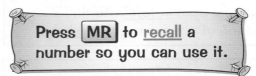 `7 6 ÷ 5 =` `15.2`

2) Now press **M+** to put 15.2 into the calculator memory.

3) Now all you need to do is type in **MR** instead of 15.2 when you do the subtraction. `5 0 − MR =` `34.8`

Brackets Tell You What to Do First

If a calculation contains brackets... **ALWAYS** do the bit inside the brackets first.

EXAMPLE: 21 ÷ (4 + 3).

You <u>usually</u> do division before addition, but the addition is in <u>brackets</u> so do it FIRST. $21 ÷ (4 + 3) = 21 ÷ 7 = 3$

If your calculator has <u>bracket keys</u>, it'll do whatever you put inside them first. So you could do the calculation above like this:

 `2 1 ÷ ( 4 + 3 ) =` `3`

> **BODMAS** helps you remember the order to do calculations:
> **B**rackets,
> **D**ivision and **M**ultiplication, (in the order they appear)
> **A**ddition and **S**ubtraction (in the order they appear).

The Square Root Button Looks Like this: √

When you <u>square</u> a number, you multiply it by itself.
E.g. 3 squared = 3 × 3 = 9.

Finding a <u>square root</u> is the reverse.
The square root of 9 is 3 and
the short way to write this is $\sqrt{9} = 3$.

> One way to find the square root of a number is to use the <u>square root button</u> on your calculator.
> You might have to press it <u>before</u> or <u>after</u> the number. Try it out on your calculator.

Learning Objective:

"I can use the memory of a calculator, bracket keys and the square root button."

Calculators

Question 1

 Dave is saving up for a bike that costs £149. He has saved up 684 five pence pieces. How much more money does Dave need to save up? Give your answer in pounds.

1 First work out how much Dave has saved up. You want the answer in <u>pounds</u>, so convert 5p to £0.05. Now <u>multiply</u> £0.05 by 684 on your calculator.

2 Put this number in the calculator <u>memory</u>.

3 Now <u>subtract</u> the amount Dave has saved from the cost of the bike. Use the <u>memory recall</u> button.

4 Write your answer with the <u>right units</u>.

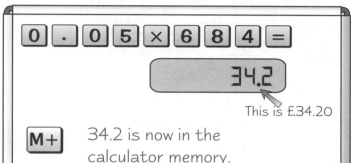

$\boxed{0}\boxed{.}\boxed{0}\boxed{5}\boxed{\times}\boxed{6}\boxed{8}\boxed{4}\boxed{=}$

$\boxed{34.2}$

This is £34.20

$\boxed{M+}$ 34.2 is now in the calculator memory.

$\boxed{1}\boxed{4}\boxed{9}\boxed{-}\boxed{MR}\boxed{=}$

$\boxed{114.8}$

Dave needs to save £114.80 more.

Question 2

 Calculate:
a) $5.8 - (6.5 + 1.2)$ b) $\sqrt{38}$ to 1 decimal place.

a If your calculator has <u>bracket keys</u>, just type this calculation in. If not, do the bit in brackets first, put it in the <u>memory</u> and subtract it from 5.8.

a) $\boxed{5}\boxed{.}\boxed{8}\boxed{-}\boxed{(}\boxed{6}\boxed{.}\boxed{5}$
$\boxed{+}\boxed{1}\boxed{.}\boxed{2}\boxed{)}\boxed{=}$

OR:
calculate 6.5 + 1.2 = 7.7 and press $\boxed{M+}$
Then do 5.8 – $\boxed{MR}$
Both methods give you –1.9.

b) 1 Use the <u>square root button</u> on your calculator to find the square root of 38.

2 <u>Round</u> the answer to the correct number of decimal places.

b) $\boxed{\sqrt{}}\boxed{3}\boxed{8}\boxed{=}$ $\boxed{6.1644140}$

6.1<u>6</u>44140

Look at the digit to the right of the decimal place you're rounding to. It's 6 here, so round up to 6.2.

$\sqrt{38}$ = 6.2

<u>Brackets first or fear the worst...</u>

So there you are. Yet more wonders of the calculator. Remember — calculators always come up with the correct answer, but only if you give them the right instructions.

Multiply and Divide by 10, 100 and 1000

Move Digits Left to Multiply by 10, 100 or 1000

If you're multiplying by 10, move the digits **ONE PLACE** to the **LEFT**.

If you multiply by 100, move the digits **TWO PLACES** to the **LEFT**.

The number of _zeros_ tells you the number of _places_ to move.

$35 \times 10 = \underline{350}$

| | 3 | 5 | . | | |
| | 3 | 5 | 0 | . |

<u>Add a decimal point</u> if there isn't one.

Fill in the empty places before the decimal point with <u>zeros</u>.

$75.9 \times 100 = \underline{7590}$

| | | 7 | 5 | . | 9 |

| 7 | 5 | 9 | 0 | . | 0 |

| 7 | 5 | 9 | 0 |

Add a zero in here as a <u>placeholder</u>.

There's no need to add zeros <u>after</u> the decimal point.

To multiply by 1000, move the digits **THREE PLACES** to the **LEFT**.

$27.1 \times 1000 = \underline{27\ 100}$

| | | | 2 | 7 | . | 1 |

| 2 | 7 | 1 | 0 | 0 | . | 0 |

| 2 | 7 | 1 | 0 | 0 |

The two gaps before the decimal point need to be filled in with zeros.

You don't need a zero here.

Move Digits Right to Divide by 10, 100 or 1000

To divide by 10 move the digits **ONE PLACE** to the **RIGHT**.

$8.6 \div 10 = \underline{0.86}$

| 8 | . | 6 | |

| | . | 8 | 6 |

| 0 | . | 8 | 6 |

You need to put a zero before the decimal point.

You might have to <u>add or remove zeros</u>.

To divide by 100 move the digits **TWO PLACES** to the **RIGHT**.

$7.5 \div 100 = \underline{0.075}$

| 7 | . | 5 | | |

| | . | | 7 | 5 |

| 0 | . | 0 | 7 | 5 |

Fill in the gaps with zeros.

To divide by 1000 move the digits **THREE PLACES** to the **RIGHT**.

$600 \div 1000 = \underline{0.6}$

| 6 | 0 | 0 | . | | | |

| | | | . | 6 | 0 | 0 |

| | | 0 | . | 6 | 0 | 0 |

<u>Add a decimal point</u>.

You can remove these zeros.

Add a zero at the start.

Learning Objective:

"I can multiply and divide a whole number or decimal by 10, 100 or 1000."

Multiply and Divide by 10, 100 and 1000

Question 1

Write down the number that is:
a) 1000 times as big as 2.63   b) one hundredth of 26

a You need to <u>multiply</u> **2.63** by **1000**.
Move the digits <u>three places left</u>.

b To find one hundredth of **26**,
<u>divide by 100</u>.
So move the digits <u>two places right</u>.

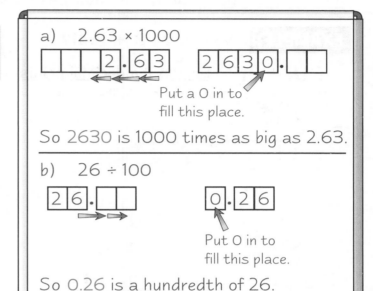

a) 2.63×1000

Put a 0 in to fill this place.

So 2630 is 1000 times as big as 2.63.

b) $26 \div 100$

Put 0 in to fill this place.

So 0.26 is a hundredth of 26.

Question 2

Suggest what the four missing digits could be
to make this calculation correct.

☐☐☐ ÷ **100 = 4.**☐

1 You know that <u>400</u> divided
by 100 would be <u>4</u>. So the
first missing digit must be **'4'**.

2 The second missing digit
can be <u>anything</u>, as long as
the last digit is the <u>same</u>.

3 The third missing digit must be
<u>zero</u>, because there are <u>no</u>
<u>hundredths</u> in the 'answer'.

4 <u>Check</u> it's right by <u>doing</u> it.

4☐☐ ÷ 100 = 4.☐

E.g.

4 3 ☐ ÷ 100 = 4. 3

4 3 0 ÷ 100 = 4. 3 0   (4.3 is the same as 4.30)

4 3 0 . ☐ ☐   ☐ ☐ 4 . 3 0

Multiplying by 1000 — shift the digits 3 places left...

Multiplying decimals by 10, 100 and 1000 is no different from multiplying whole numbers
by 10, 100 and 1000. Just keep the decimal point still and move the digits over it.

Written Adding and Subtracting

Adding Decimals — Line up the Decimal Points

You use the same column method to add both whole numbers and decimals.
Line the columns up first, then add them starting with the column of least place value.

EXAMPLE: What is 24.8 + 5.41?

```
T U . t h
  2 4 . 8
+    5 . 4 1
_____
       . 1
```

Line up the decimal points and put one in the answer.

1 Add the hundredths.

2 Add the tenths.

8 tenths + 4 tenths
= 12 tenths

```
T U . t h
  2 4 . 8
+    5 . 4 1
_____
       . 2 1
          ¹
```

Put 2 tenths in the tenths column.

10 tenths = 1 unit

3 Add the units.

4 + 5 + 1 = 10

```
T U . t h
  2 4 . 8
+    5 . 4 1
_____
   0 . 2 1
   1 1
```

Write the 0 in the units column.

10 units = 1 ten

4 Add the tens.

```
T U . t h
  2 4 . 8
+    5 . 4 1
_____
 3 0 . 2 1
   1 1
```

Remember the extra 10.

So the answer is 30.21

Subtract Decimals by Exchanging

> This is the same as the method for subtracting whole numbers.

EXAMPLE: Find the difference between 16 and 93.5.

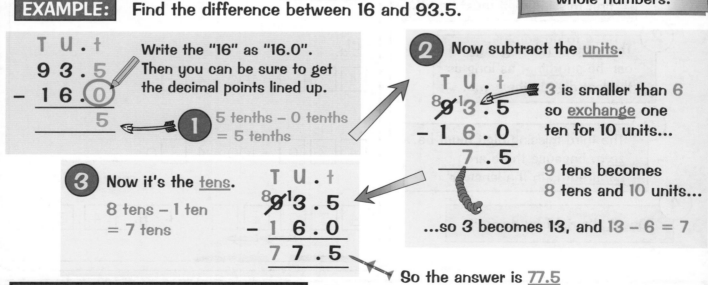

```
T U . t
  9 3 . 5
- 1 6 . 0
_____
       5
```

Write the "16" as "16.0". Then you can be sure to get the decimal points lined up.

1 5 tenths – 0 tenths
= 5 tenths

2 Now subtract the units.

```
T U . t
  ⁸9̸ ¹3 . 5
-  1 6 . 0
_____
       7 . 5
```

3 is smaller than 6 so exchange one ten for 10 units...

9 tens becomes 8 tens and 10 units...

...so 3 becomes 13, and 13 – 6 = 7

3 Now it's the tens.

8 tens – 1 ten
= 7 tens

```
T U . t
  ⁸9̸ ¹3 . 5
-  1 6 . 0
_____
  7 7 . 5
```

So the answer is 77.5

Learning Objective:

"I can add and subtract whole numbers and decimals using efficient written methods."

Written Adding and Subtracting

Question 1

Katie has £45.81 in her purse. She buys a cycling helmet for £13.89, a bell for £3.35 and some gloves for £12.30. How much money does she have left in her purse?

1 First work out how much Katie spent. Add up £13.89 + £3.35 + £12.30. Write the prices in columns, lining up the decimal points. Add up the hundredths first.

```
  13.89
   3.35    = 14 hundredths
+ 12.30    = 1 tenth + 4 hundredths
    . 4
   1       write the tenth under the tenths column
```

2 Next add up the tenths.

```
  13.89
   3.35    = 15 tenths
+ 12.30    = 1 unit + 5 tenths
   .54
  1 1       write the unit under the units column
```

3 Then add the units, then the tens.

```
  13.89        13.89
   3.35         3.35
+ 12.30      + 12.30
   9.54        29.54
   1 1          1 1
```

Katie spent £29.54

4 Now work out how much Katie has left. Subtract £29.54 from £45.81. Line up the decimal points again. Subtract the hundredths first — you need to do some exchanging.

```
  45.8¹1    1 hundredth is smaller than
- 29.54     4 hundredths, so exchange
    . 7     1 tenth for 10 hundredths.
```

5 Next subtract the tenths.

```
  45.⁷8¹1
- 29.54
   .27
```

6 Then subtract the units, then the tens.

Exchange 1 ten for 10 units.

```
  ³4⁵5.⁷8¹1        ³4⁵5.⁷8¹1
-  29.54        -  29.54
    6.27           16.27
```

7 Write the answer with the correct units.

Katie has £16.27 left.

Line the decimal points up — or it'll be a complete flop...

It's easy to make a slip when you're adding and subtracting, so do an estimate first to check your answer is sensible. Try rounding the amounts above and estimating the answer.

Written Multiplying and Dividing

Multiplying by a One-Digit Integer

Remember:
Integer just means
a whole number.

1) Write out the calculation with the <u>big number on top</u>.
Line up the place value columns.

2) Multiply the <u>one-digit</u> number by <u>each part</u> of the big number in turn.
Start with the place value column of <u>least</u> value (it's always the one on the right).

3) Each time you get an answer of 10 or more, <u>record</u> the first digit
of the answer below the next column (like you do when you're adding).

EXAMPLE: Work out 167 × 4 without using a calculator.

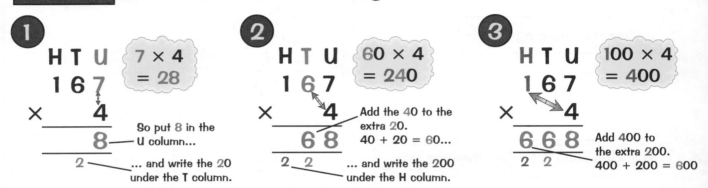

①

```
  H T U
  1 6 7
×     4
───────
      8
  2
```

7 × 4
= 28

So put 8 in the
U column...

... and write the 20
under the T column.

②

```
  H T U
  1 6 7
×     4
───────
    6 8
  2 2
```

60 × 4
= 240

Add the 40 to the
extra 20.
40 + 20 = 60...

... and write the 200
under the H column.

③

```
  H T U
  1 6 7
×     4
───────
  6 6 8
  2 2
```

100 × 4
= 400

Add 400 to
the extra 200.
400 + 200 = 600

Dividing by a One-Digit Integer

This method is known as <u>short division</u>. It's great for dividing by a <u>one-digit integer</u>.

1) <u>Partition</u> the big number into hundreds, tens and units.
Divide each of these numbers, starting with the <u>highest</u> place value.
(It's different from adding, subtracting and multiplying.)

2) Put the <u>result</u> of each division <u>on top</u> in the correct place value column.

3) Sometimes you need to exchange. This example shows you how.

EXAMPLE: What is 392 ÷ 7?

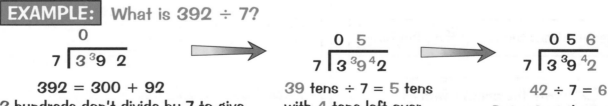

```
    0
7 ⟌ 3 ³9 2
```

392 = 300 + 92
3 hundreds don't divide by 7 to give
any hundreds. So put 0 at the top.
<u>Exchange</u> 3 hundreds for 30 tens.

```
    0 5
7 ⟌ 3 ³9 ⁴2
```

39 tens ÷ 7 = 5 tens
with 4 tens left over.
Put 5 on top. Exchange
the 4 tens for 40 units.

```
    0 5 6
7 ⟌ 3 ³9 ⁴2
```

42 ÷ 7 = 6
Put a 6 at the top and we're
done. The answer is <u>56</u>.

Learning Objective:

"I can multiply and divide whole numbers
by one-digit integers."

Written Multiplying and Dividing

Question 1

Mr Smith buys a sun hat for each child in a school. There are 576 children in the school. Sun hats are sold in packs of 8 and each pack costs £6. How much does Mr Smith spend?

1 Work out how many packs of sun hats Mr Smith needs. You need to divide the number of children (576) by the number of sun hats in a pack (8).

Partition 576 into 5 hundreds + 7 tens + 6. Try to divide 5 hundreds by 8.

You've exchanged the 5 hundreds for tens so you now have 57 tens. Divide them by 8.

You had 1 ten left which you exchanged for 10 units. Now there are 16 units. Divide them by 8.

2 You need to find the cost of 72 packs of hats. So multiply 72 by the cost of one pack. Write this as a calculation.

First multiply 2 by 6.

Then multiply 70 by 6.

Write the answer out with the correct units.

Mr Smith needs 576 ÷ 8 packs of hats.

5 hundreds don't divide by 8 to give any hundreds.

So put 0 on the top and exchange 5 hundreds for 50 tens.

$$8\overline{)5^57\,6}$$

57 tens ÷ 8 = 7 tens with 1 ten left over.

Exchange the 1 ten for 10 units.

$$8\overline{)5^57^1\,6}$$

16 ÷ 8 = 2

$$8\overline{)5^57^16}$$ 576 ÷ 8 = 72

So, 72 packs of hats are needed.

Mr Smith spends 72 × £6.

$$\begin{array}{r} 72 \\ \times\ 6 \\ \hline 2 \\ 1 \end{array}$$ $2 \times 6 = 12$

Put 2 in the units column...
... and write the 10 under the tens column.

$$\begin{array}{r} 72 \\ \times\ 6 \\ \hline 432 \\ 1 \end{array}$$ $70 \times 6 = 420$

Add the 20 to the extra 10.
20 + 10 = 30
... and put the 400 in the hundreds column.

Mr Smith spends £432.

Partition 3-digit numbers so you can divide them...

These methods are all about exchanging. If you understand what you're doing, then you'll have a better chance of remembering how to do multiplication and division like this.

Written Multiplying and Dividing

Partition to Multiply by Two-Digit Numbers

Multiplying by two-digit numbers looks tricky, but if you <u>partition</u> the number, it's not so bad.

EXAMPLE: What is 246 × 34?

You need to <u>partition</u> the number 14: 14 = 10 + 4.
Work out 246 × 30 and 246 × 4 <u>separately</u>, then <u>add them together</u>.

STEP 1

First find 246 × 4.
See page 28 if you've forgotten how to do this.

```
 Th H T U
    2 4 6
 ×      3 4
    9 8 4
    1 2
```

246 × 4 = 984
Write the answer here as usual.

STEP 2

Now find 246 × 30.
Write the answer here.

```
 Th H T U
    2 4 6
 ×      3 4
    9 8 4
  7 3 8 0
  1 1
```

Boris always had trouble with Step 2.

STEP 3

Add to get the final answer.

```
 Th H T U
    2 4 6
 ×      3 4
    9 8 4
 + 7 3 8 0
  8 3 6 4
```

Use Chunking to Divide by Two-Digit Numbers

With this method, you keep <u>subtracting multiples</u> of the two-digit number until none are left.

EXAMPLE: What is 305 ÷ 13?

1 <u>3 hundreds</u> don't divide by 13 to give any hundreds.
So put 0 at the top and <u>exchange</u> the 3 hundreds for <u>30 tens</u>.

```
        0
 13 | 3³0 5
```

2 There are <u>30 tens</u>. So find the multiple of 13 that is close to but just less than <u>30 tens</u>.
13 × 1 ten = 13 tens
13 × 2 tens = 26 tens
13 × 3 tens = 39 tens — too high
So 13 × 2 tens = 26 tens is the one you want.
Put the 2 tens on top and subtract 26 tens from 305.

```
     0 2
 13 | 3³0 5
   − 2 6 0
     4 5
```

Put the 2 tens in the tens place.

← 13 × 2 tens = 26 tens

← You've got 45 left.

3 There's <u>45 left</u> to be divided now. So find the multiple of 13 that is close to but just less than <u>45</u>.
13 × 2 = 26
13 × 3 = 39
13 × 4 = 52 — too high
So 13 × 3 = 39 is the one you want.
Put the 3 on top and subtract 39 from 45.

```
     0 2 3
 13 | 3³0 5
   − 2 6 0
     4 5
   −   3 9
       6
```

Put the 3 in the units place.

← 13 × 3 = 39

← You've got 6 left.

4 There's only <u>6 left</u> now. It's too small to divide by 13 to give a whole number. So it's the <u>remainder</u>.

```
     0 2 3 r6
 13 | 3³0 5
```

So, the answer is <u>23 r6</u>.

Learning Objective:

"I can multiply and divide a three-digit integer by a two-digit integer."

Written Multiplying and Dividing

Question 1

Rachel uses 756 g of cheese to make 21 pies. Each pie is one-sixteenth cheese.
What is the mass of each pie?

1 Work out how much cheese is in each pie. Divide **756 g** by **21**.

7 hundreds won't divide by **21** to give any hundreds. So exchange the 7 hundreds for **70 tens**. There are now **75 tens**.

Now find the **multiple of 21** that's close to but just less than **75 tens**. It's **21 × 3 tens = 63 tens**. Put the 3 tens at the top.

Subtract **63 tens** from **756**. There's **126** left to divide.

126 is an exact multiple of **21**. **21 × 6 = 126**. Put the 6 at the top.

Read the **answer** at the **top**.

2 So, $\frac{1}{16}$ of a pie has a mass of 36 g.

So **multiply** 36 g by 16 to find the mass of one whole pie.

First multiply 36 by 6.

Then multiply 36 by 10...

...and add the products.

Finally, write out the answer with the **correct units**.

Cheese in each pie = 756 g ÷ 21

7 hundreds won't divide by 21 to give any hundreds, so 0 goes here.

$$21 \overline{)7\,^{7}5\ 6}\ ^{0}$$

7 hundreds = 70 tens

$$
\begin{array}{r}
0\ 3\ 6 \\
21\overline{)7\,^{7}5\ 6} \\
-\ 6\ 3\ 0 \\
\hline
1\ 2\ 6 \\
-\ 1\ 2\ 6 \\
\hline
0
\end{array}
$$

← 21 × 3 tens = 63 tens
← 21 × 6 = 126
← Nothing left to divide.

So each pie contains 36 g of cheese.

Mass of one pie = 36 g × 16

$$
\begin{array}{r}
3\,6 \\
\times\ 1\,6 \\
\hline
6 \\
\end{array}
$$
6 × 6 = 36

$$
\begin{array}{r}
3\,6 \\
\times\ 1\,6 \\
\hline
2\,1\,6 \\
\end{array}
$$
3 tens × 6 = 18 tens

Add the 18 tens to the extra 3 tens. This gives 21 tens.

$$
\begin{array}{r}
3\,6 \\
\times\ 1\,6 \\
\hline
2\,1\,6 \\
3\,6\,0 \\
\end{array}
$$
6 × 10 = 60
3 tens × 10 = 300

$$
\begin{array}{r}
3\,6 \\
\times\ 1\,6 \\
\hline
2\,1\,6 \\
+\,3\,6\,0 \\
\hline
5\,7\,6
\end{array}
$$

Each pie has a mass of 576 g.

Multiply by 2 digits — × the units, × the 10s, add...

When you're multiplying using the written method shown here, you work from right to left. But when you're dividing, you work from left to right. It's just what makes things easier.

Written Multiplying and Dividing

Multiplying Decimals

One of the numbers you have to multiply might be a <u>decimal</u>.
You can use the method for multiplying whole numbers (see page 28)...
...but with a clever <u>twist</u>.

EXAMPLE: What is 1.92 × 3?

First do a whole-number
calculation, 192 × 3 ⟶

```
    1 9 2
  ×     3
  ─────────
    5 7 6
      2
```

It's always a good idea to <u>estimate</u> before you do the real multiplication.
1.92 × 3 ≈ 2 × 3 = <u>6</u>

BUT <u>192</u> is <u>100 times</u> as big as <u>1.92</u>.
So the answer to 192 × 3 will be <u>100 times too big</u>.

so divide by 100

576 ÷ 100 = <u>5.76</u>

Dividing Decimals

Dividing a <u>decimal</u> is OK too. Do a <u>whole-number</u> calculation first, then adjust.

EXAMPLE: What is 19.2 ÷ 6?

<u>Estimate</u> first again:
19.2 ÷ 6 ≈ 18 ÷ 6 = <u>3</u>

Work out <u>192 ÷ 6</u>. The answer will be <u>10 times bigger</u> than 19.2 ÷ 6, so <u>divide it by 10</u>.

192 ÷ 6 ⟶

```
    0 3 2
  6 ) 1 ¹9 ¹2
```
= 32 ⟶

32 ÷ 10 = 3.2
So 19.2 ÷ 6 = <u>3.2</u>

Learning Objective:

"I can multiply and divide decimals by a one-digit integer."

Written Multiplying and Dividing

Question 1

Sam is making 7 netball skirts for the school team. Each skirt needs 1.42 m of fabric. He has 10 m of fabric. How much will he have left over?

1 First work out how much fabric is needed for 7 skirts.
You need to find <u>1.42 × 7</u>.
It's easier to work out <u>142 × 7</u>, then adjust.

2 142 is 100 times as big as **1.42**.
This means the answer to **142 × 7** will be <u>100 times too big</u>. So <u>divide</u> it by 100.

3 You're not finished yet.
You have to <u>subtract</u> the length of fabric needed from <u>10 m</u>.

142 × 7:

$$\begin{array}{r} 1\ 4\ 2 \\ \times\quad 7 \\ \hline 9\ 9\ 4 \\ \scriptstyle 2\ 1 \end{array}$$

142 × 7 = 994

1.42 × 7 = 994 ÷ 100 = 9.94

9.94 m of fabric is needed to make 7 skirts.

10 m – 9.94 m = 0.06 m

0.06 m of fabric was left over.

Question 2

There is 8.56 g of salt in a packet of 8 sausage rolls. Kayley eats one sausage roll and a bag of crisps containing 3.2 g of salt. How much salt does she eat?

1 First work out how much salt is in one sausage roll. You need to find <u>8.56 ÷ 8</u>. It's easier to work out <u>856 ÷ 8</u>, then adjust.

2 856 is 100 times as big as **8.56**.
So, the answer to **856 ÷ 8** will be <u>100 times too big</u>. So <u>divide</u> it by 100.

3 Now <u>add</u> on the salt that she ate in the bag of crisps.

$$\begin{array}{r} 1\ 0\ 7 \\ \hline 8\ |\ 8\ 5^5 6 \end{array}$$

<u>Estimate:</u>
sausage roll ≈ 8 g ÷ 8 = 1 g
crisps ≈ 3 g
1 + 3 = <u>4 g</u>

856 ÷ 8 = 107

8.56 ÷ 8 = 107 ÷ 100 = 1.07

There's 1.07 g of salt in each sausage roll.

1.07 + 3.2 = 4.27

Kayley ate 4.27 g of salt.

The point is — get the decimal point in the right place...

This is a crafty way of multiplying and dividing decimals. It's good to <u>estimate</u> first. If your final answer is much bigger or smaller than your estimate, you probably adjusted wrongly.

Practice Questions

1   Kim mixes apple juice, honey and lemonade together to make 1275 ml of a new drink.

   a)   Three sevenths of the new drink is lemonade.
        How many ml of lemonade did she use? Give your answer to the nearest ml.

   b)   37% of the new drink is apple juice.
        How many ml of apple juice did she use? Give your answer to the nearest ml.

2   A museum has 1179 skulls. Four ninths are mammal skulls and 86 are bird skulls.
     The rest are reptile skulls.

     How many reptile skulls are there?

3   Write down the answers to the calculations below.

                   A 1000 − (160 × 0.4)   **B** 975 ÷ (50 + 490)

                   C (1000 − 160) × 0.4   **D** (975 ÷ 50) + 490

4   Calculate these square roots. Give your answers to 2 decimal places.

   a) $\sqrt{63}$

   b) $\sqrt{197}$

5   Copy and complete these multiplications and divisions.

   a)   56 ÷ 100 = ☐

   b)   1000 × 0.21 = ☐

   c)   10 × ☐ = 0.5

   d)   45 ÷ ☐ = 0.045

Practice Questions

6   Louise and Ben go to the garden centre.
     Louise buys a rose bush for £8.75, a palm tree for £19.59 and a plant pot for 61p.

   a)   She pays with two twenty pound notes. How much change does she get?

   b)   Ben spends £15.89 on lunch for them. How much less does Ben spend than Louise?

7   A normal year is 365 days and a leap year is 366 days.
     Olivia is 7 years old today. There has been one leap year since she was born.

   How many days has Olivia been alive for?

8   There are 316 children at Grizebeck Primary School.

   a)   Mrs Khan divides all the children into four equal teams.
         How many children are in each team?

   b)   All the children in the school go ice skating. 9 teachers go with them.
         Entry costs £3 for each child and £5 for each teacher.
         How much does the trip cost in total?

9   Paul makes rocking chairs. He sells the rocking chairs for £288 each.

   a)   One year Paul sells 43 rocking chairs.
         How much money does he get in total that year?

   b)   Every time Paul sells a rocking chair he celebrates by spending one twelfth of the
         money he gets on bacon. How much does he spend on bacon each time he sells
         a chair?

10   A teacher buys 2.58 kg of mince for a cookery class.

   a)   The mince costs £8 per kg. How much change does the teacher get from £25?

   b)   The mince is shared between 6 children in a cookery class.
         How many grams of mince does each child get?

Angles

You Can *Estimate Angles*

You can estimate how big an angle is by comparing it to one of these.

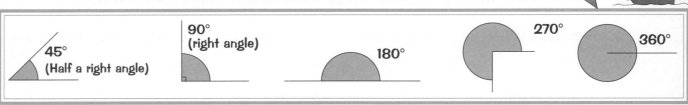

45°
(Half a right angle)

90°
(right angle)

180°

270°

360°

Decide if your angle is a <u>bit smaller</u> or <u>larger</u> than one of these, then adjust your estimate.

EXAMPLES:

This angle is bit less than 90°.
I'd estimate that it's 80°.

> This is an <u>acute angle</u>.
> Acute angles are less than 90°.

This is about a right angle
and a half. If you ask me,
I'd say it's about 135°
(90° + 45° = 135°).

> This is an <u>obtuse angle</u>. Obtuse angles are
> more than 90° but less than 180°.

You Can Use a *Protractor to Measure Angles...*

① Put the <u>cross on the</u>
<u>protractor</u> over the
<u>vertex</u> of the angle.

② <u>Line up</u> the <u>bottom line on</u>
<u>the protractor</u> with one line
of your angle.

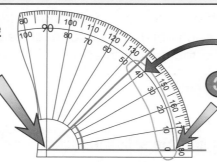

③ Just <u>read</u> the scale.
Use the scale that has <u>0</u>
on the line of your angle.
The angle is <u>45°</u>.

...and Draw Angles too

EXAMPLE: Draw an angle of 81°.

① Draw a line.

② Put the cross on the protractor
over one end of the line. Line up
the bottom line on the protractor
with the line you've drawn.

③ Make sure you're using the scale
that starts at <u>0</u> on the line. Mark
the paper above 81° with a dot.

④ Then just join a straight line
between the end of the line and
the dot.

> Don't forget to
> label the angle.

81°

Learning Objective:

"I can estimate angles, and use a protractor
to measure and draw them."

Angles

Question 1

Look at the angle on the right.
Circle the approximate size of this angle.

60°   90°   110°   160°   190°

1 Compare the angle to a <u>right angle</u> (90°) and a <u>straight line</u> (180°).

2 Cross out the angles on the list that it <u>can't</u> be.

3 Now decide between the sizes that are left.

> The angle is bigger than a right angle, but smaller than a straight line.
>
> It's more than 90° but less than 180°.
>
> ~~60°~~   ~~90°~~   110°   160°   ~~190°~~
>
> So it could be 110° or 160°.
>
> The angle is a little bit more than 90°. So it's about 110°.
>
> (160° is nearly a straight line.)
>
> 60°   90°   (110°)   160°   190°

Question 2

Measure the angle marked a.
Use a protractor.

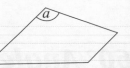

1 Position the <u>protractor</u> correctly:
- the protractor's cross should be on the vertex of the angle you're measuring,
- line up the bottom line of the protractor with one line of the angle.

(Here, you'll need to <u>rotate the page</u> so you can measure the angle easily.)

2 Read from the scale that <u>starts with zero</u>.

3 Check your answer is <u>sensible</u>.

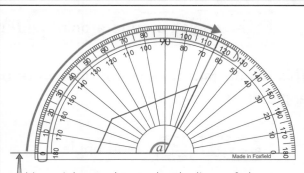

> You might need to make the lines of the angle longer.
>
> a = 115°
>
> The angle is more than 90° but less than 180°. So 115° is sensible.

Use a protractor to draw and measure angles...

When you're drawing and measuring angles, be absolutely sure you're measuring <u>from 0</u> on the protractor. Get into the habit of estimating the angle to check you're about right.

Calculating Angles

Remember the 180° Triangle Fact

> All the angles in a triangle add up to 180°.

You can use this amazing fact to work out the missing angles in triangles.

EXAMPLE: This is an equilateral cheese triangle. Work out the sizes of angles y and z.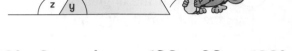

It's an equilateral triangle so all three angles inside the triangle are equal.

So <u>angle y</u> will be 180 ÷ 3 = <u>60°</u>.
Angles y and z make up a <u>straight line</u>. That's <u>180°</u>. So <u>angle z</u> = 180 − 60 = <u>120°</u>.

ANOTHER EXAMPLE

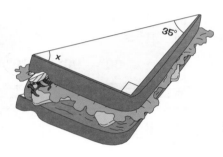

Not drawn accurately

Find the angle x on the bee and blue cheese sandwich.

35° + 90° + x = 180°.
So x = 180° − 35° − 90° = <u>55°</u>

Also Remember the 360° Angles-at-a-Point Fact

> The angles around a point add up to 360°.

This also means the angle at the centre of a circle is 360°.

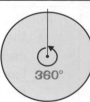

This handy fact means you can work out a missing angle around a point.

EXAMPLE: Find angle k.

You know all the angles must add up to 360°.
90° + 90° + 110° + k = 360°

Subtract the angles from 360° to find angle k.
So k = 360° − 110° − 90° − 90° = <u>70°</u>

Learning Objective:

"I know that the angle sum of a triangle is 180° and the sum of angles around a point is 360°."

Calculating Angles

Question 1

Dave measures some of the angles on his bike frame.
Calculate the size of angle **a**.

1 You know that the angles in a triangle add up to <u>180°</u>.

2 <u>Subtract</u> the two known angles from 180° to find angle **a**.

3 <u>Check your answer</u> by adding all three angles together.

$58° + 74° + a = 180°$

$a = 180° - 58° - 74° = 48°$
So angle a is 48°.

Check: $58° + 74° + 48° = 180°$
The three angles make 180° so it's right.

Question 2

Find the angle between the minute hand and the hour hand of a clock at 7pm.

1 There are <u>360°</u> in a full circle. They are divided into 12 sections by the numbers on the clock.

2 Work out how many degrees there are in <u>each section</u>.

3 Work out how many degrees there are <u>between the hands</u>.

4 Check your answer by estimating...
This angle is a bit less than <u>two right angles</u>, which would be $2 \times 90° = \underline{180°}$. So the answer looks about right.

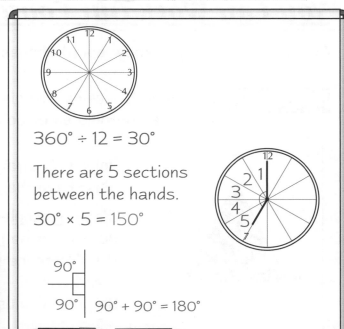

$360° ÷ 12 = 30°$

There are 5 sections between the hands.
$30° \times 5 = 150°$

90°
90° $90° + 90° = 180°$

Remember 180° and 360° — they're important...

You need to memorise these two angle facts — the angles in a triangle total 180°, and the angles around a point total 360°. Then you just need to do a bit of calculating.

Coordinates

A Point is Identified by its Coordinates

A point has two numbers to identify its position: its <u>coordinates</u>.

Coordinates tell you how many <u>across</u> and how many <u>up or down</u> from (0, 0) a point is.

They're always put in <u>brackets</u> like this: (8, 9).

Make sure you put the x and y coordinates in the right order. You always go <u>across first</u>.

The <u>coordinates</u> of the points opposite are:

A(1, 1)	C(–4, –3)
B(–2, 3)	D(3, –1)

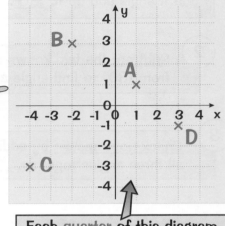

By the way, to save saying "the point (0, 0)" all the time, you call this the <u>origin</u>.

Each <u>quarter</u> of this diagram is called a <u>quadrant</u> — there are 4 quadrants altogether.

You Can Work Out Coordinates

You can use what you know about shapes to work out coordinates.

EXAMPLE: This is an isosceles triangle. Sides AB and BC are equal. Find the coordinates of point <u>C</u>.

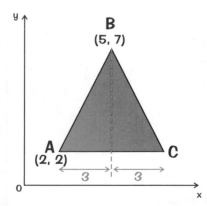

Point C is straight <u>across</u> from point A, so it must have the <u>same y-coordinate</u> as A. That's <u>2</u>.

It's an <u>isosceles</u> triangle so it's symmetrical. So B must be <u>halfway</u> across the triangle. The difference between the x-coordinates of A and B = 5 – 2 = 3. So point C must have the x-coordinate 5 + 3 = <u>8</u>.

So C's coordinates must be <u>(8, 2)</u>.

Learning Objective:

"I can use coordinates in all four quadrants."

Coordinates

Question 1

The shaded shape on the right is a parallelogram.
The coordinates of points A, B and C are given.
Find the coordinates of point D.

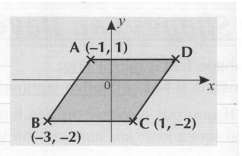

1 Look to see whether point D is in a <u>horizontal or vertical line</u> with any other point. This can give you the x- or y-coordinate.

Point D is in line horizontally with Point A — so they have the same y-coordinate. It's 1.

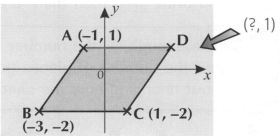

2 Next, think about what you know about the shape — the <u>opposite sides</u> of parallelograms are <u>equal lengths</u>.

Side AD is the same length as side BC.

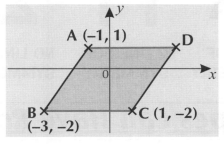

3 Now use this information to find the <u>x-coordinate</u> of D.

The x-coordinate of B is −3 and the x-coordinate of C is 1.
So C is 4 units to the right of B.

D must be 4 units to the right of A.
The x-coordinate of A is −1, and
−1 + 4 = 3. So the x-coordinate of D is 3.

4 Write the <u>pair of coordinates</u> and <u>check</u> it is sensible.

D (3, 1) ← This is sensible. D is in the part of the grid where both coordinates are positive.

You must get the coordinates in the right order...

The horizontal coordinate always goes first, even for negative coordinates.
Remember, you always go along the corridor (↔) before going up (or down) the stairs (↕).

Symmetry

2D Shapes Can Have Line Symmetry

This shape has a <u>mirror line</u>.
This means it has <u>reflective symmetry</u>.

Mirror line

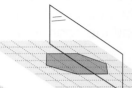

If you put a mirror on this line,
it looks like you can see the <u>whole shape</u>.

There Can be More Than One Line of Symmetry

If you can draw <u>two</u> mirror lines you say there are <u>two</u> lines of symmetry.
If you can draw <u>three</u>, you say there are <u>three</u> lines of symmetry, and so on.
If you can't draw <u>any</u>, then there are <u>no</u> lines of symmetry.

> Simple enough — the number of lines of symmetry
> is just the number of places you can put a mirror
> without changing how the shape looks.

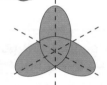

| 1 LINE OF SYMMETRY | 2 LINES OF SYMMETRY | NO LINES OF SYMMETRY | 1 LINE OF SYMMETRY | 3 LINES OF SYMMETRY | NO LINES OF SYMMETRY |

Shapes Can Have Rotational Symmetry Too

<u>ROTATIONAL SYMMETRY</u> is where you can <u>rotate</u> the shape or drawing into different positions that all look <u>exactly</u> the same.

> Rotating a shape just means turning it.

<u>Order of rotational symmetry</u> is a fancy way of saying:
"how many times the shape <u>fits into itself</u> when it is turned through 360".

EXAMPLES:

Order 1
(or no rotational symmetry)

Order 2

Order 3

Order 4

Learning Objective:

"I can identify all the symmetries of 2D shapes."

Symmetry

Question 1

a) Which shapes below have **three lines of reflective symmetry**?
b) Which shapes below have **rotational symmetry of order 2**?

A   B   C   D   E   F

a

Work out how many <u>lines of symmetry</u> each shape has. If you're not sure, trace the shape and <u>fold</u> it to check. (If the two sides <u>match up</u> perfectly, the line you folded along was a line of symmetry.)

b

Work out the <u>order of rotational symmetry</u> of each shape. If you're not sure, <u>trace</u> the shape and turn the tracing through 360°, counting how many times the traced shape fits exactly into the shape itself.

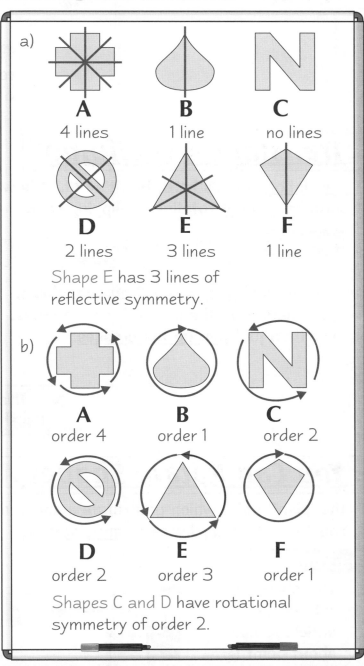

a)

A — 4 lines   B — 1 line   C — no lines

D — 2 lines   E — 3 lines   F — 1 line

Shape E has 3 lines of reflective symmetry.

b)

A — order 4   B — order 1   C — order 2

D — order 2   E — order 3   F — order 1

Shapes C and D have rotational symmetry of order 2.

There are different types of symmetry...

A shape with rotational symmetry <u>of order 1</u> really has <u>no</u> rotational symmetry (which is a bit confusing). Reflective symmetry is a bit easier: think about <u>folding</u> to make matching halves.

Transformations

Reflection in a Line

You can <u>reflect</u> shapes in a mirror line.

> Each <u>point</u> and its <u>reflection</u> are exactly the <u>same distance</u> from the mirror line.

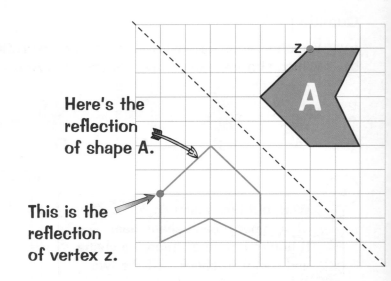

Here's the reflection of shape A.

This is the reflection of vertex z.

Translation is Sliding

<u>Translation</u> sounds hard, but it's not. It's when a shape <u>slides</u> from one place to another, <u>without</u> rotating or flipping over.

EXAMPLE Translate the green shape 3 squares down and 1 square to the left.

For <u>each vertex</u>, go 3 squares down, 1 square to the left and mark a cross. Then just <u>join up the crosses</u>.

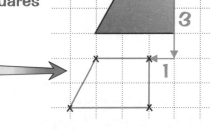

This is <u>not</u> a translation. The shape has <u>turned</u> as well.

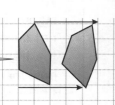

You Can Rotate Shapes About a Point

The 'pivot' point which you rotate a shape about is called the <u>centre of rotation</u>. You can rotate <u>clockwise</u> or <u>anticlockwise</u>.

EXAMPLE:

This shape is rotated 90° anticlockwise about point S.

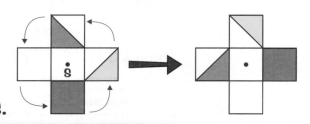

Clockwise is the same way clock hands turn. Guess what... anticlockwise is the other way.

Clockwise:

Learning Objective:

"I can reflect, translate and rotate shapes."

Transformations

Question 1

Katherine translated a shape 2 squares up and 3 squares right.
Her answer is shown on the grid.
Draw the position of the **original shape** on the grid.

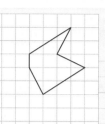

1 The shape on the grid is the translated shape. You need to find the <u>original shape</u>. So you need to <u>reverse</u> the translation.

2 Do the <u>reverse translation</u>. Translate each vertex *3* left and *2* down and mark them with crosses. Join up the crosses to draw the original shape.

3 <u>Check</u> you're right by doing the translation from the original shape to Katherine's shape.

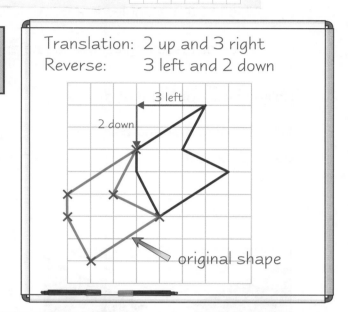

Translation: 2 up and 3 right
Reverse: 3 left and 2 down

3 left

2 down

original shape

Question 2

Rotate shape A **90° anticlockwise** about point O.
Label the new shape **B**.

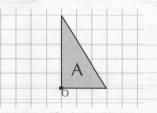

A

O

1 Trace the shape <u>and</u> the centre of rotation. Press a pencil on the <u>centre of rotation</u> to hold the tracing paper in place.

2 Look at the <u>horizontal</u> line on shape A. You need to do <u>a 90° turn</u>, so turn the tracing paper anticlockwise until the line becomes vertical.

<u>If it was a 180° turn</u>, you'd turn your tracing paper until the line was horizontal again.

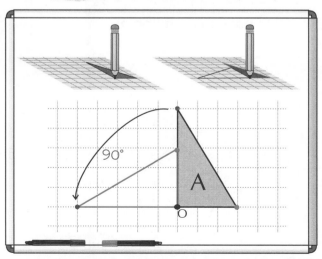

90°

A

O

You're going to need a sharp pencil for all this...

The key to these questions is reading the question really, really carefully. Check if it says anticlockwise or clockwise, and which point you're rotating about. In fact, check twice.

Practice Questions

1   Four angles are shown below.

a)   Which of these angles is approximately 190°?

b)   Which of these angles is an acute angle?

2   Sally draws a diagram of a house.

Measure angles **A** and **B**.
Use a protractor.

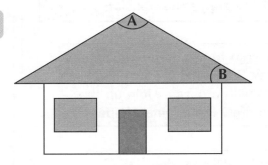

3   Look at the flag shown on the left.

Calculate the angle labelled z.
Do not use a protractor.

4   Darcey makes the spinner on the right.

Calculate the angle marked X.
Do not use a protractor.

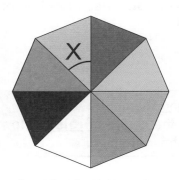

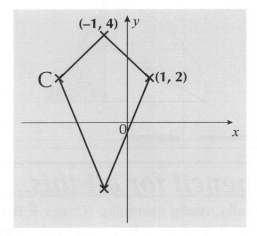

5   Jack draws the kite on the left.

Work out the coordinates of point C.

Practice Questions

6   This shape is made up of 7 identical squares.

   a)   How many lines of symmetry does this shape have?

   b)   What is this shape's order of rotational symmetry?

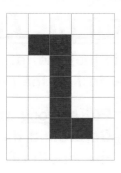

7   Copy this shape onto a grid.

   a)   Reflect the shape in the mirror line.

   b)   Label the reflection of vertex P.

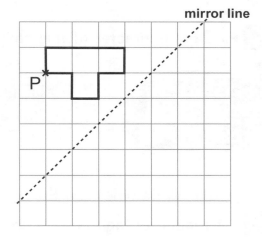

8   Kelly draws a shape on a grid and labels it A.

She then translates this shape and labels the new shape B.

What translation did Kelly use?

9   Copy this shape onto a grid.

Rotate the shape 90° clockwise about vertex A.

Draw the square in its new position. Include the circle in your drawing.

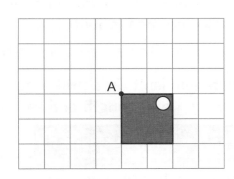

Calculating Perimeter and Area

Finding the Perimeters of Shapes

Perimeter is just the total distance around the outside of a shape.
Here's how to find the perimeter of a shape:

1) Put a cross at one corner.
2) Go around the shape, adding up the length of every side.
3) Keep going until you get back to the cross, then stop.

You might need to work out 'missing lengths' before you can add them up.

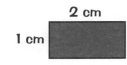

Rectangles have 2 pairs of equal sides. So the missing sides must be 1 cm and 2 cm.

EXAMPLE: Find the perimeter of this shape:

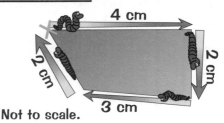

Not to scale.

Using a cross, and going around the shape, the answer is 4 + 2 + 3 + 2 = 11 cm.

If a shape is regular all its sides are the same length.

EXAMPLE: A regular octagon has 5 cm sides. Find its perimeter.

It's a regular octagon so it has 8 sides, all 5 cm long.
So its perimeter is 8×5 cm = 40 cm.

Area of Rectangles — Just Multiply

Count how many squares long the rectangle is.
Then count how many squares wide it is.
Then multiply these numbers together.

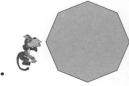

I am the Count and I like to count squares. Von, two, three...

EXAMPLE: Work out the area of this slightly interesting rectangle.

There are 3 rows of 6 square centimetres in this rectangle. So the area is just $3 \times 6 = 18$ cm².

This just means 18 square centimetres.

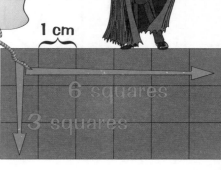

1 cm

6 squares

3 squares

If a rectangle isn't on a grid, you can just measure its length and width.

Area = length × width

Learning Objective:

"I can solve problems involving perimeter. I can find the area of a rectangle using area = length × width."

Calculating Perimeter and Area

Question 1

Susan's garden is a rectangle measuring 4 metres by 5 metres. She wants to put a fence around the outside. Susan has 15 metres of fencing. Does she have enough?

1 Work out all the <u>side lengths</u>.

2 <u>Add</u> up all the side lengths to find the perimeter. Remember to answer the question too.

> It's a rectangle, so it will have two pairs of equal sides. Two sides will measure 4 m and two sides will measure 5 m.
>
> Perimeter = 4 + 4 + 5 + 5 = 18 metres. So Susan doesn't have enough fencing.

Question 2

The diagram shows a room in Dave's house.
a) Calculate its perimeter.
b) Calculate its area.

a) 1 Work out the <u>missing lengths</u>.

2 Go around the shape, <u>adding</u> up the side lengths.

b) 1 <u>Break the shape up</u> into two rectangles. Use the side lengths to find their areas.

2 <u>Add together</u> the areas of the two rectangles to find the <u>total area</u> of the room.

a) $5 \text{ m} - 3 \text{ m} = 2 \text{ m}$

$3 \text{ m} - 1 \text{ m} = 2 \text{ m}$

$5 + 3 + 3 + 2 + 2 + 1 = 16 \text{ m}$
So the perimeter is 16 m.

b)

$A = 1 \times 2$
$= 2 \text{ m}^2$
$B = 3 \times 3$
$= 9 \text{ m}^2$

$2 \text{ m}^2 + 9 \text{ m}^2 = 11 \text{ m}^2$

Find the missing lengths — look under the sofa...

Perimeters and areas are both to do with the side-lengths of your shape. You add them up to find the perimeter or multiply the length by the width to find the area of a rectangle.

Units and Measures

There are Lots of Units for Length

There are 4 units of length you need to know.

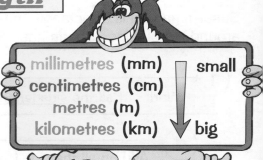

10 mm = 1 cm   100 cm = 1 m
1000 m = 1 km

millimetres (mm)   small
centimetres (cm)
metres (m)
kilometres (km)   big

EXAMPLE: Write the correct unit in this sentence:
The length of a pencil is about 16 ___.

ANSWER: Millimetres are too small.
Metres and kilometres are too large.   Centimetres (cm) are about right.

Use a Balance or Scales to Find Mass

You measure mass on a balance or weighing scales.
The units of mass are kilograms (kg) and grams (g).

Kilo means 1000 of something.
1 kilogram = 1000 grams

EXAMPLE: Circle one amount to make this sentence correct.

"An apple has a mass of about: 100 kg   10 kg   (100 g)   10 g "

↖ too big ↗
(A small dog is
about 10 kg.)

↑ too small
(That's about right for
two sheets of paper.)

Capacity is How Much a Container Can Hold

Liquids have a volume. This is the amount of space they take up.
The largest volume of liquid a container can hold is called its capacity.

You can measure capacity in
millilitres (ml) and litres (l).

"Milli" means $\frac{1}{1000}$.
There are 1000 millilitres in a litre.
1000 ml = 1 l

EXAMPLE: Circle the most likely capacity of a teaspoon.

0.5 ml   (5 ml)   50 ml   5 l   50 l

↑
too small
(This is about the volume of a raindrop.)

too big
(A washing-up bowl holds about 5 litres.)

Learning Objective:

"I can choose appropriate units to measure length, mass
and capacity. I can make estimates in everyday contexts."

Units and Measures

Question 1

Suggest a suitable unit for measuring the following things:

a)   the volume of water in a bath
b)   the mass of a pen
c)   the height of a building

1 Imagine each thing — think about how big or small it is.

2 Find a unit that isn't <u>too big</u> or <u>too small</u>.

a)   Millilitres would be too small.
<u>Litres</u> is more sensible.

b)   Kilograms would be too big for just one pen.
<u>Grams</u> would be better.

c)   Millimetres and centimetres would be far too small.
Kilometres would be too big.
<u>Metres</u> is sensible here.

Question 2

A box holding 35 pencils has a mass of ½ kg.
The box has a mass of 52 g when it is empty.

Calculate the mass of one pencil to the nearest gram.

1 The mass of a pencil will be a few <u>grams</u>. So make sure all the measurements you use are in grams too.

2 Find the mass of the 35 pencils <u>without the box</u>. You have to <u>subtract</u>.

3 Now you can find the mass of <u>one pencil</u>. You have to <u>divide</u>.

4 Remember to <u>round</u> the answer to the nearest whole number and put the right <u>unit</u> in your answer.

The mass of the full box is ½ kg.
1 kg = 1000 g so ½ kg = 500 g.

500 g – 52 g = 448 g

448 g ÷ 35 = 12.8 g

12.8 rounds up to 13.
So the mass of one pencil is approximately 13 g.

Always use the most sensible unit...

When you're measuring something, always use an appropriate unit. It'd be a bit silly to measure the height of a bus in millimetres, or the mass of an elephant in grams...

Units and Measures

Sometimes You Need to Convert Units

EXAMPLE: Bucket A has a capacity of 6.2 l. Bucket B has a capacity of 6300 ml. Which bucket can hold more wormy sludge?

Put both capacities into the same units.

> 1 litre = 1000 ml

So to convert l to ml, multiply by 1000.

Bucket A's capacity = 6.2 × 1000 = 6200 ml

6300 ml is more than 6200 ml.
So Bucket B can hold more wormy sludge.

EXAMPLE: Larry can jump 1.8 m. Kyle can jump 20 centimetres further. How far can Kyle jump in centimetres?

You need to give your answer in centimetres, so convert all the units into centimetres.

> 1 m = 100 cm

So 1.8 m = 1.8 × 100 cm = 180 cm.
So Kyle can jump 180 cm + 20 cm = 200 cm.

EXAMPLE: Ruby's mass is shown on the scales to the right. What is Ruby's mass in kilograms?

The difference between two numbered marks
is 1000 g – 800 g = 200 g.
There are 10 divisions between each numbered mark.
So each division shows 200 g ÷ 10 = 20 g.
Ruby's mass is 1000 – 20 – 20 – 20 = 940 g.

You need to convert
940 g into kilograms.

> 1 kg = 1000 g

So 940 g = 940 ÷ 1000
= 0.94 kg

Learning Objective:

"I can convert larger units into smaller units."

Units and Measures

Question 1

Alice has 2.4 litres of lemonade. Arthur has 2600 millilitres.
How much more lemonade does Arthur have than Alice?

1 You need to convert both volumes into the <u>same units</u>.

2 Convert both to <u>millilitres</u>. Multiply the litres by 1000.

3 Find the difference between Alice and Arthur's volumes by <u>subtraction</u>.

2.4 litres   2600 millilitres

2.4 × 1000 = 2400 ml

2600 ml – 2400 ml = 200 ml
So Arthur has 200 ml more.

Question 2

One portion of cereal is shown on the scales.
How many portions are there in a 360 g box of cereal?

1 Work out what <u>each division</u> on the scale is worth.

2 Read the scale to find out the <u>mass of one portion</u>.

3 <u>Divide</u> 360 g by the mass of one portion of cereal to find the <u>number of portions</u>.

There are 5 divisions between 0 and 50, so each division shows 50 ÷ 5 = 10 g.

The arrow points to 4 divisions above 0, so one portion is 4 × 10 = 40 g.

360 ÷ 40 = 9 portions

Convert from large to small units by multiplying...

You need to remember that 1 litre = 1000 ml, 1 metre = 100 cm and 1 kilogram = 1000 g.
And when you've done a conversion, always <u>check</u> to see if your answer is <u>sensible</u>.

Units and Measures

Units Can be Metric or Imperial

Metric units are used more commonly now than imperial units.
Some people still use imperial units though — I bet your parents or grandparents do.

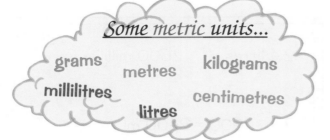

Some metric units...

grams   metres   kilograms
millilitres   centimetres
litres

Some imperial units...

miles   inches   pints
feet   ounces   yards

You Can Convert Between Metric and Imperial

You can convert imperial units to metric units, or the other way round.
For example, you could change a distance in feet to a distance in metres.

Make sure you know these common conversions:

1 metre ≈ 3 feet
1 kilogram ≈ 2 pounds
1 litre ≈ 2 pints
8 kilometres ≈ 5 miles
100 grams ≈ 4 ounces

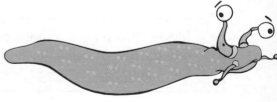

The sign '≈' means 'is approximately equal to'. These conversions aren't exact but it's fine to use them for rough calculations.

EXAMPLE: James finds a 5 metre long slug.
Approximately how long is the slug in feet?

Step 1)   Find the conversion fact you need: here it's 1 metre ≈ 3 feet.

Step 2)   Every 1 metre is 3 feet, so you will have 3 times as many feet as metres.
So you need to multiply by 3.

$$5 \times 3 = 15$$

Step 3)   So the slug is approximately 15 feet long.

Learning Objective:

"I can convert roughly between imperial and metric units."

Units and Measures

Question 1

Ali is making a cake.
The recipe says that she needs **half a pound** of sugar.
Which bag of sugar should she buy to make this cake?

0.5 kg   1 kg   2 kg

1 You need to remember the right conversion fact. The question is about kilograms and pounds.

2 Use the conversion fact to convert half a pound into metric units.

3 So Ali needs 250 g of sugar. Work out which bag would be the most suitable.

1 kilogram ≈ 2 pounds

2 pounds ≈ 1 kg
1 pound ≈ 1 kg ÷ 2 = 500 g
½ pound ≈ 250 g

0.5 kg = 500 g. This would be enough.
The other bags would both be too much.
So she should buy the 0.5 kg bag.

Question 2

Peter is driving from Leeds to Manchester.
The distance is about 40 miles.
Approximately how far is this in kilometres?

1 Write down the conversion fact for miles and kilometres.

2 Use the conversion fact to change 40 miles into kilometres.

5 miles ≈ 8 kilometres.

40 miles is <u>8 lots</u> of 5 miles.
That's equal to about <u>8 lots</u> of 8 km.
8 × 8 km = 64 km

Metric units are replacing imperial units...

You need to <u>learn</u> the conversion facts. Then you can work out and compare distances, masses and capacities. You might find imperial masses in a cake recipe. Mmmm, cake...

Practice Questions

1   Arthur's field is a rectangle that measures 20 metres by 15 metres.
    He wants to put a fence around the outside.

    Arthur has 60 metres of fencing.
    Will he have enough? Show your working.

2   Matthew's classroom is rectangular. It measures 8 metres by 6 metres.

    a)   Calculate the perimeter of the classroom.

    b)   Calculate the area of the classroom.

3   Tasha draws a diagram of her bedroom.

    a)   Calculate its perimeter.

    b)   Calculate its area.

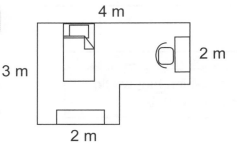

4   Ash's garden measures 4 metres by 5 metres.
    His garden has a pond that measures 2 metres by 3 metres.

    Calculate the area of Ash's garden that surrounds the pond.

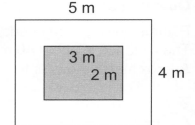

5   Robert wants to make some clothes. He has two pieces of material.
    One measures 6 metres by 7 metres. The other measures 8 metres by 9 metres.

    Calculate the total area of the material.

6   Estimate some measurements for the following things. Use suitable **metric** units.

    a)   The volume of a bucket of water.

    b)   The mass of an egg.

    c)   The length of a car.

Practice Questions

7   A box of chocolates contains 25 chocolates and has a mass of 100 g.
The empty box has a mass of 25 g.

Calculate the mass of one chocolate.

8   Write the following masses in order, from smallest to largest.

2 kg   20 g   2 g   2500 g   2.4 kg

9   Alice cycled 5.6 km. Paul cycled 5100 metres.

Who cycled further?

10   Donald needs 2 kg of flour.
The scales show how much he has already.

How many more grams of flour does he need?

11   Beth is 126 cm tall. Anne is 1.31 m tall.

By how many centimetres is Anne taller than Beth?

12   Susan has 3.5 metres of ribbon.

a)   How many centimetres is this?

b)   Approximately how many feet is this?

13   Sun-Yi is driving to visit her friend. The journey is 72 km.

How far is this in miles?

Chance and Likelihood

Probability is How Likely Something Is

The <u>probability scale</u> goes from 0 to 1. If something is impossible, the probability is <u>0</u>. If it is certain, the probability is <u>1</u>.

```
                                    Coin landing on heads
                                              ↓
0   Scoring 6 when you roll a dice.    Even    I will eat breakfast tomorrow.   1
```

You normally describe probability using <u>fractions</u>.
Imagine that you have <u>10 frog counters</u> in a bag. You pick one without looking.

7 of the 10 counters are <u>orange</u>, so you have a <u>7 out of 10</u> chance of getting an orange counter.

This probability is $\frac{7}{10}$ (which you could convert to <u>0.7</u> or <u>70%</u>).

<u>The probability</u> of getting a counter with a <u>frog</u> on is <u>1</u>. They've all got frogs on so you are certain to get a frog one.

The probability of getting a counter with a <u>penguin</u> on is <u>0</u>. (There are <u>no</u> penguin counters so it's impossible to get one.)

Hmph.

Probabilities can Change

The outcome of one action can <u>affect the probability</u> of later actions.

EXAMPLE: Scott asks Jill and then John to randomly pick a <u>chocolate</u> from a box of 10. There are <u>6 orange</u> chocolates and <u>4 toffee</u> chocolates.

Jill picks first...

The <u>probabilities</u> for <u>Jill</u> of choosing each type of chocolate are:

Orange = $\frac{6}{10}$ Toffee = $\frac{4}{10}$

Jill takes an <u>orange</u> chocolate and eats it.

...then John picks

The probabilities for <u>John</u> are <u>different</u> because:
1.   There are now only <u>5 orange</u> chocolates left.
2.   There are still <u>4 toffee</u> chocolates left.
3.   There are now only <u>9</u> chocolates <u>in total</u>.

The chances for <u>John</u> are:

Orange = $\frac{5}{9}$ Toffee = $\frac{4}{9}$

Learning Objective:

"I can find and justify probabilities using fractions, decimals and percentages."

Chance and Likelihood

Question 1

Look at these two spinners.

Explain why you are more likely to spin a 1 on A than B.

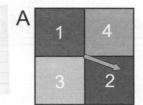 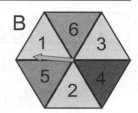

① **Write down the number of <u>possible</u> <u>outcomes</u> on each spinner.**

② **Work out the probability of getting a <u>1 on each spinner</u>.**

③ **Use these probabilities to <u>write an explanation</u>.**

There are 4 equal sections on spinner A, so 4 equally likely outcomes. On spinner B there are 6 equally likely outcomes.

<u>Spinning 1 on A</u>:
There are 4 possible outcomes and only one is a 1. So the probability is ¼.

<u>Spinning 1 on B</u>:
There are 6 possible outcomes and only one is a 1. So the probability is ⅙.

1 out of 4 is a greater chance than 1 out of 6 so you are more likely to spin a 1 on A.

Question 2

There are 12 balls in a bag. The scale below shows the probability that a ball taken from the bag at random is **blue**.

a) How many blue balls are in the bag?

b) 2 blue balls are taken out and not put back.
What is the probability now of getting a blue ball when one ball is taken at random?

```
0                              ↑        1
```

a **Look at the <u>probability scale</u>. The probability of taking a blue ball is $\frac{3}{4}$, so $\frac{3}{4}$ of the balls in the bag must be blue.**

b) ① **Work out <u>how many balls are left</u> and how many of them are <u>blue</u>.**

② **Use the <u>new totals</u> to work out the new probability.**

a) Three quarters of 12
= 12 ÷ 4 × 3 = 9
There are 9 blue balls in the bag.

b) There would be 12 − 2 = 10 balls left in the bag in total.
There would be 9 − 2 = 7 blue balls.

New probability = $\frac{7}{10}$ or 0.7 or 70%

Probability is a scale from 0 to 1...

Remember, a probability of 0 means that an event is impossible. As you go up the scale, events are more and more likely to occur... and then 1 means that something is certain.

Analysing Data

The Mode is the Most Common Value

To work out the mode:

1) Write all the numbers down in <u>order of size</u>.
2) Find the <u>number</u> that appears <u>most often</u> in your list. This number is the <u>mode</u>.

There can be <u>more than one</u> mode.

EXAMPLE: Five people each recorded how many pies they could eat in 12 hours. This list shows the results. ⟹ 1, 3, 3, 5, 9

The number <u>3</u> appears <u>twice</u>, but <u>1, 5 and 9</u> only appear <u>once</u>.

So the <u>mode</u> is 3 pies.

The Median is the Middle Value

To work out the median:

1) Write all the numbers down in <u>order of size</u>.
2) The number in the <u>middle</u> of your list is the <u>median</u>.

When there are <u>two</u> <u>middle numbers</u> the median is <u>halfway</u> <u>between</u> them.

EXAMPLE: What is the median height in this list?
2.3 m, 1.8 m, 2.7 m, 2.0 m, 0.9 m, 1.6 m

Arrange the heights in <u>order</u>: 0.9 m, 1.6 m, (1.8) m, (2.0) m 2.3 m, 2.7 m.
Find the <u>middle position</u>: halfway between 1.8 m and 2.0 m.

So the <u>median height</u> is <u>1.9 m</u>.

The Mean Involves Adding and Dividing

To work out the mean:

1) <u>Add up</u> all the numbers.
2) <u>Divide</u> the total by <u>how many</u> numbers there are.

The mean is often just called the "<u>average</u>". If someone asks, "What's the average of these tiddlywink scores?" they probably want to know the <u>mean</u>.

EXAMPLE: Sam throws the following scores on a dartboard:
3, 12, 18, 21, 40, 56.

The total of all these throws is 3 + 12 + 18 + 21 + 40 + 56 = 150.
There are six scores so you divide by 6.
His <u>mean</u> score is 150 ÷ 6 = <u>25</u>.

Learning Objective:

"I can solve problems using mode, median and mean."

Analysing Data

Question 1

a) Write a number in each of these boxes so that the mode of the five numbers is 15.

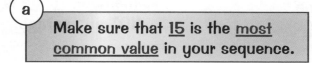

b) What is the median of your numbers?

a

Make sure that <u>15</u> is the <u>most common value</u> in your sequence.

b

The median is the <u>middle value</u> when the numbers are <u>in order</u>. So put the numbers in size order.

a) Your numbers could be:

b) In order: 4, 7, 8, 15, 15
The middle number is in the third position.
In this case the median is 8.

Question 2

Rob throws a javelin ten times. These are the distances he throws in metres.

| 42.4 | 44.7 | 42.5 | 43.6 | 46.8 |
| 47.1 | 43.0 | 44.2 | 42.4 | 45.3 |

What is the mean (average) distance?

1

To work out the mean, first you <u>add up</u> all the results.

2

Then you <u>divide</u> the total by the <u>number of results</u> you added together.

The total of all the results is:
42.4 + 44.7 + 42.5 + 43.6 + 46.8 + 47.1 + 43.0 + 44.2 + 42.4 + 45.3
= 442

There are 10 results. So divide by 10:
442 ÷ 10 = 44.2.

The mean distance is 44.2 metres.

Use mode, median and mean to analyse data...

Don't get your averages confused. Remember, the <u>MO</u>de is the <u>MO</u>st common number.
The me<u>D</u>ian is the mi<u>DD</u>le one. And the <u>mean</u> is the hardest (<u>mean</u>est) to work out.

Analysing Data

The Range is Biggest – Smallest

> In other words, the range is the **difference** between the biggest and smallest numbers.

To Work Out the Range

1) Write all the numbers down in order of size.
2) Subtract the smallest number from the biggest number. The answer is the range.

> Remember, range is **NOT** an average.

EXAMPLE: Find the range of these numbers: 12 30 9 17 3 16

Put the numbers in size order: 3 9 12 16 17 30

30 is the biggest number and 3 is the smallest. So the range = 30 – 3 = **27**.

You can Use Averages to Compare Data

Sometimes it's hard to compare sets of data just by looking at them.
It can be a lot easier if you work out the ranges or averages.

EXAMPLE: Compare Sally's and Carl's maths test scores for each term. Who do you think is better at maths?

① You could say that Sally is better at maths because she has the highest test score.

Sally: 12   34   92
Carl: 51   54   57

③ Sally has a mean score of 46. Carl's mean score is 54. So I would say Carl is better at maths because his mean score is higher.

② But you could say Carl is better at maths because his scores have a smaller range than Sally's. Carl always does OK, while Sally does badly in some tests and really well in others.

EXAMPLE:

Adi and Jim have a sprout throwing contest. They throw 5 sprouts each and measure the distance of each throw.

	Sprout 1	Sprout 2	Sprout 3	Sprout 4	Sprout 5
Adi	210 cm	234 cm	252 cm	198 cm	226 cm
Jim	205 cm	187 cm	263 cm	214 cm	230 cm

The person with the highest mean distance wins. Who wins overall?

Adi's mean distance thrown = 1120 cm ÷ 5 = 224 cm
Jim's mean distance thrown = 1099 cm ÷ 5 = 219.8 cm

224 cm is further than 219.8 cm, so **Adi** wins.

Learning Objective:

"I can compare sets of data using different averages and the range."

Analysing Data

Question 1

This table shows the score for each member of two teams in a spelling competition.
Which team was better at spelling?
Use the **mean** and **range** to explain your answer.

Team A: 1, 2, 2, 3, 6, 9, 9, 9, 9, 10

Team B: 6, 6, 6, 6, 6, 6, 7, 8, 8, 8

1 Work out the <u>range</u> and the <u>mean</u> for both sets of scores.

Range: Team A = 10 – 1 = 9
         Team B = 8 – 6 = 2
Mean: Team A: 1 + 2 + 2 + 3 + 6 + 9 +
         9 + 9 + 9 + 10 = 60
    So Team A's mean score = 60 ÷ 10 = 6
         Team B: 6 + 6 + 6 + 6 + 6 +
         6 + 7 + 8 + 8 + 8 = 67
    So Team B's mean score = 67 ÷ 10 = 6.7

2 Use the mean and range to <u>explain</u> which team you think is better.

Team B is better at spelling. They have a higher mean score and a smaller range of scores, which shows they are more consistent.

Question 2

Work out the mean, median, mode and range of the following numbers:

7, 10, 8, 5, 17, 8, 19, 15, 13, 22, 8

1 First put the numbers <u>in order</u>.

2 You can find the <u>mode</u> and <u>median</u> quite quickly.

3 Subtract the <u>smallest number</u> from the <u>largest</u> to find the <u>range</u>.

4 To get the <u>mean</u>, divide the <u>total</u> of the numbers by <u>how many</u> there are.

In order, the numbers are:

5, 7, 8, 8, 8, 10, 13, 15, 17, 19, 22

The mode is 8.
It's the most
common number.

The median is 10
because it's the
middle value.

Range = 22 – 5 = 17

Total of numbers: 132
There are 11 numbers.
Mean = 132 ÷ 11 = 12

I would say this is average, but that'd be mean...

If a question asks you to <u>explain</u> something about a set of numbers, don't just work out the mean, median or mode and then stop. You need to say clearly what your calculations <u>show</u>.

Tables and Charts

You have to <u>display</u> data so that it's easy to understand.
There are lots of ways to do this (charts, tables, graphs). Pick the best way for your data.

You can Show Grouped Data on a Bar Chart

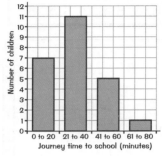

This bar chart shows the <u>journey times to school</u> for one class.
The vertical axis could also be labelled <u>frequency</u>.

QUESTION: How many children have journeys longer than 40 minutes?

ANSWER: 6 children (just add the frequencies of the 41-60 and 61-80 bars)

Interpreting Line Graphs

I heated up a pie and then put it outside in the snow.
This line graph shows the <u>temperature</u> of my pie as it cooled down.

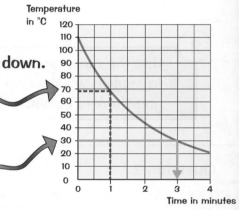

You can see that after <u>1 minute</u>, the temperature was about <u>69 °C</u>.

How long did it take for the pie to cool to 30 °C?

Find 30 °C on the vertical axis. Read across to the line, then down. You get <u>3 minutes</u>.

Pie Charts show things as Proportions

Bertie Entwhistle spends <u>6 hours</u> at work every day.
This <u>pie chart</u> shows how he spends his time at work.
Each coloured slice is called a "<u>sector</u>".
The <u>size</u> of each <u>sector</u> tells you <u>how much of his time</u> he spends doing different things.

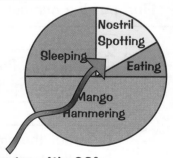

You can work out how long Bernie spends <u>Nostril Spotting</u>.

1) <u>Measure the angle</u> for the nostril-spotting sector using a protractor. It's 60°.

2) Work out <u>what fraction</u> that is of the whole pie chart.
   A circle is 360°, so you divide by 360. $60° \div 360° = \frac{1}{6}$

3) The whole pie chart shows 6 hours. So Bertie nostril-spots for $\frac{1}{6}$ of 6 hours.

$$\frac{1}{6} \times 6 \text{ hours} = \underline{1 \text{ hour}}$$

Learning Objective:

"I can represent data in different ways and understand its meaning."

Tables and Charts

Question 1

Nancy runs a cracker-eating competition for her class at school.
She displays the results in a bar chart.

a)   How many children are in Nancy's class?

b)   What fraction of the children ate 3 or more crackers in 2 minutes?

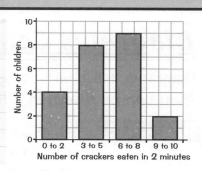

a

To work out how many children are in Nancy's class, <u>add the frequencies of all the bars</u> together.

a)   The 0 - 2 column represents 4 children.
     The 3 - 5 column represents 8 children.
     The 6 - 8 column represents 9 children.
     The 9 - 10 column represents 2 children.
     4 + 8 + 9 + 2 = 23 children.

b) **1**

Find the <u>number of children</u> who ate **3** or more crackers.

2

Write this as a <u>fraction</u> of the total number of children.

b)   It's the last three bars:
     8 + 9 + 2 = 19 children.

     So the fraction of children
     who ate 3 or more crackers was $\frac{19}{23}$.

Question 2

Liam asked 42 people to pick their favourite fruit from a choice of 5. How many more people chose bananas than melons?

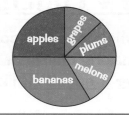

1

<u>Measure the angles</u> for the bananas and melons sectors.

Measured angle of bananas sector = 120°.
Measured angle of melons sector = 60°.

2

Find the <u>fraction of people</u> who chose bananas and melons. Then use this to find the <u>number of people</u> who chose each.

The fraction of people who chose bananas
= 120 ÷ 360 = $\frac{1}{3}$
So $\frac{1}{3}$ of 42 people chose bananas. 42 × $\frac{1}{3}$ = 14

The melons sector is <u>half</u> the size of the banana sector. So 14 ÷ 2 = 7 people chose melons.

3

Work out the <u>difference</u>.

14 – 7 = 7, so 7 more people chose bananas.

98% of people wish that pie charts were actually pies...

Charts and graphs are much easier to make sense of than horrible long lists of numbers. With pie charts, you often have to measure angles. Make sure you do it accurately.

66

Conclusions

Diagrams Can Be Misleading

Diagrams like charts or graphs can be misleading.
They can be drawn in different ways to make the data look different.

EXAMPLE: Judith draws two graphs. They both show the sales of dragons at her Dragon shop over 6 years. The same data has been used to draw both graphs.

Judith likes to use the second graph. It makes the increase in dragon sales look bigger.

This zig-zag bit means that part of the axis has been missed out to save space.

The rest of the numbers are more spread out. The line is stretched out vertically, so it looks steeper.

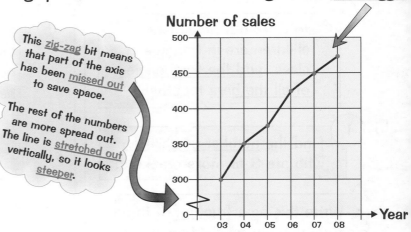

Draw Conclusions and Ask Other Questions

The whole point of collecting data and making charts or graphs is to answer a question, like this one.

How long does it take most pupils to get to school?

1) So look carefully at the diagram, and work out what the data tells you. This is called drawing conclusions.

The most common journey time is 21-40 minutes.

This is a conclusion.

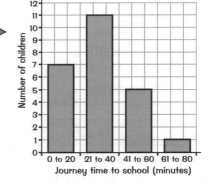

2) When you've drawn your conclusion, think about what you could do better next time. Maybe you could ask more people, or split the data into more groups.

3) Think about what other questions you could investigate. For example, are pupils' journey times shorter the nearer to school they live?

Learning Objective:

"I can use my results to solve problems."

SECTION SIX — HANDLING DATA

Conclusions

Question 1

Richard is running in a race.
He records the total distance he has run every minute during the first 10 minutes.

Time (minutes)	1	2	3	4	5	6	7	8	9	10
Distance (km)	0.2	0.4	0.5	0.7	0.8	0.9	0.9	1.1	1.2	1.4

a) Use the data to plot a line graph of his run.
b) Suggest what might have happened between minutes 6 and 7 on the graph.

a)

1 Number the axes in even jumps, making sure your scale is sensible. You want the distance scale to go up to about 1.5 km so that all the points fit on the graph.

2 Remember to give your graph a title, and to label both the axes.

3 Plot the points from the table and use a ruler to join them together.

b)

1 Look at the shape of the graph between 6 and 7 minutes.

2 Think what Richard must have done to cause this.

The graph looks like this:

A graph to show the distance run by Richard

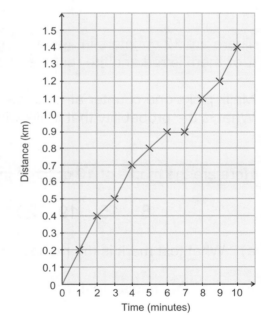

The graph is flat between 6 and 7 minutes. This means Richard's distance doesn't change for a minute.

Richard must have stopped. He might have stopped for a rest or to tie his shoe-lace.

Graphs aren't much use unless you can read them...

If you're drawing a graph, make sure your axes go up to the highest numbers that you need to plot. If you're reading from a graph check the scale really carefully (and the units).

Practice Questions

1   Look at these two spinners.

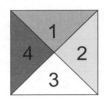   

Ashley's spinner   Kelly's spinner

a)   Kelly says, "We both have the same chance of spinning a 2."
Explain why she is correct.

b)   Ashley says, "We both have the same chance of spinning an odd number."
Explain why he is wrong.

2   There are 12 counters in a bag. 3 of them are blue,
1 of them is red and the rest are green.

Malik picks one counter at random.
What is the probability that Malik will pick a green counter?

3   Here are the marks of 10 children in a geography test.

8   15   19   20   16   12   13   9   12   18

a)   What test mark is the mode?

b)   Find the median test mark.

4   Write down three numbers that have a mean of 6.

5   Bob and Dave have a swimming competition. They both swim 50 m five times.

    Here are their times in seconds.

Bob: 30.2   32.1   34.1   31.2   34.0

Dave: 30.1   31.5   33.6   35.0   30.5

a)   Whose times have the greater range?

b)   The person with the faster mean time wins. Who wins?

Practice Questions

6   Dara jumps as far as she can 10 times. Here are her distances in metres.

   1.2   0.9   1.3   1.5   1.0   1.2   1.1   1.0   1.2   1.3

   What is her mean distance jumped?

7   This bar chart shows the number of hours of sunshine per day for two weeks.

   a)   How many more hours of sunshine were there on Tuesday of week 1 than on Tuesday of week 2?

   b)   Find the median number of hours of sunshine in week 1.

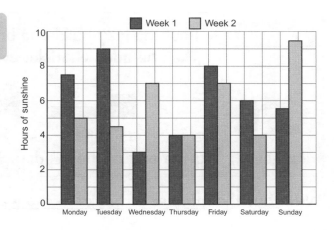

8   72 people were asked to choose their favourite sport. The results are shown in this pie chart.

   How many people chose tennis?

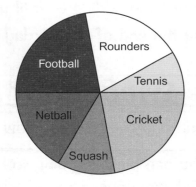

9   A shop keeper records how many jumpers she sells each month.

   a)   How many jumpers were sold in October?

   b)   Suggest a reason why the number of jumpers sold increases between August and November.

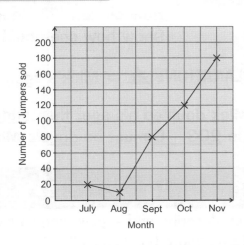

Number Patterns

You Always Need to *Find a Rule*

It's always the same with number patterns and sequences.

<u>Work out the rule</u> for getting from one term to the next.

> Every number or shape in a sequence is called a '<u>term</u>'.

After that, you just use the rule to answer the question.

EXAMPLE: Paul the lazy builder is building a wall. He lays 4 bricks on day 1. Then he adds 3 bricks every day.

 1st day 2nd day 3rd day

Paul says, "By the end of the 6th day, the wall will have 20 bricks." Is he right?

Write out the <u>number of bricks in the wall</u> each day as terms in a <u>sequence</u>.

> 4, 7, 10, ...   You're just <u>adding 3</u> more bricks each day.

So just keep adding 3 until you get to the <u>6th</u> <u>term</u>. ⟶ 4, 7, 10, 13, 16, 19, ...

So by the end of the 6th day the wall will have 19 bricks. So Paul is <u>wrong</u>.

Use *Symbols* for Numbers You *Don't Know*

You can <u>use symbols</u> to show numbers <u>you don't already know</u>.

You can pick <u>anything</u> to be a symbol: a square, a letter, a giraffe... Just remember to <u>say what it stands for</u>.

EXAMPLE: Mick says, "If I <u>double</u> my age and <u>add five</u> I get the answer 203. How old am I?" Jane works out the answer: "Mick is 99." Show how she could have worked it out.

EXPLANATION: △ = Mick's age.

Mick doubled his age, then <u>added 5</u> to get 203. So <u>203 – 5</u> must be <u>double</u> Mick's age.

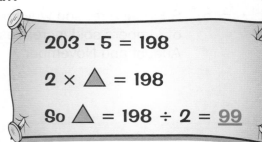

$$203 - 5 = 198$$
$$2 \times \triangle = 198$$
$$\text{So } \triangle = 198 \div 2 = \underline{99}$$

Learning Objective:

"I can describe and explain sequences, patterns and relationships."

Number Patterns

Question 1

Claire writes a sequence starting at –45. She adds the same number each time:

−45, −32.5, −20...

Write the next two numbers in the sequence.

1 Work out <u>what number</u> is being added each time.

2 Work out the <u>fourth</u> number in the sequence by <u>adding 12.5</u>.

3 Then work out the <u>fifth</u> number — <u>be careful</u> when you go past <u>zero</u>.

Find the difference between −45 and −32.5.

−32.5 − (−45) = <u>12.5</u>

Check this with the second pair of terms:

−20 −(−32.5) = <u>12.5</u>

−20 + 12.5 = −7.5

−7.5 + 12.5 = 5

Question 2

Peter is making patterns using grey and white tiles.
The number of **grey** tiles he uses in each pattern
is **four less** than **six times** the pattern number.
How many grey tiles will Peter use
in pattern **number 16**?

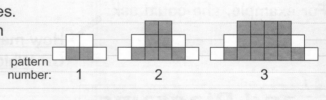

pattern number: 1   2   3

1 Choose a <u>symbol</u> to stand for the pattern number — say "<u>n</u>".

2 Write "four less than six times the pattern number" as a number sentence.

3 Work out the answer when <u>n = 16</u>.

4 Write your answer <u>in words</u>.

n = pattern number

(6 × n) − 4

(6 × 16) − 4 = 96 − 4 = 92

Peter will use 92 grey tiles.

Number patterns are all about finding a rule...

Using symbols to stand for numbers you don't know yet is a really good trick.
You'll use symbols in a lot of maths lessons from Year 7... so you might as well start now.

Planning Problem Solving

Data Can be Organised in Tables...

EXAMPLE: Jess wants to know what sports school children take part in. Suggest how she might go about investigating this.

Jess could start by <u>asking her friends what sports they take part in</u>.

When Jess asked her friends what sports they played, she collected this data.

Kate	Shaz	Jake	Hannah	Bill	Lucy	Kim	Lauren
football and hockey	netball	netball	rounders	rounders and football	none	football	football

This isn't very well organised. You can't see clearly how many people play each sport.

Jess could use the information to make a <u>tally chart</u>.

This is <u>much better</u>. You can see that <u>more people play football than any other sport</u>.

	Tally	Total
hockey			1
football						4
netball				2
rounders				2

Think how Jess could <u>extend</u> her investigation. For example, she could ask:

<u>How many hours of sport do you play a week?</u>
OR <u>Which is your least favourite school sport?</u>

...and Diagrams

You need to be able to draw and interpret diagrams and charts.

Always <u>read the scales on bar charts and line graphs carefully</u>. 1 grid square up doesn't always mean an increase of 1.

Remember the mode of a data set is the most common value. So on a bar chart it will have the <u>highest bar</u>.

E.g. the mode flavour of ice cream sold is <u>chocolate</u>.

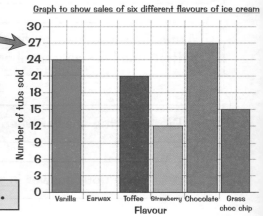

Graph to show sales of six different flavours of ice cream

Learning Objective:

"I can suggest a line of enquiry and plan how to investigate it."

Planning Problem Solving

Question 1

The diagram shows a game board.

To play, you choose a set of three touching hexagons. Two possible sets are marked on the board.

To find your score, you multiply together the numbers on the three hexagons.

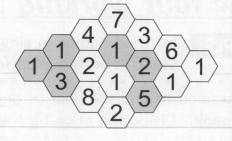

a)   What is the highest possible score?

b)   Dan scores 56. Mark on the board the three hexagons he chooses.

c)   Write two more questions you could ask about the numbers on the board.

---

1   Before you start, decide how you're going to solve the problem.

2   You're looking for the highest possible score, so try all the sets with 8 in and all the sets with 7 in.

3   Make a table so that you can record your findings clearly. This also means that you're less likely to miss out any combinations.

4   Look back at your table to see if there's a score of 56 anywhere to answer part b).

5   Now think of two more questions to ask. You can base your questions on the ones you're given...

6   ...or ask something completely different.

set	score	set	score
8, 1, 1	8	7, 1, 1	7
8, 1, 2	16	7, 1, 2	14
8, 1, 5	40	7, 1, 3	21
8, 2, 2	32	7, 1, 4	28
8, 2, 3	48	7, 3, 2	42
8, 2, 4	64	7, 3, 6	126
8, 2, 5	80	7, 4, 2	56
8, 3, 1	24	7, 4, 3	84

a)   The highest possible score is 126.

b)   Dan chooses 7, 4 and 2.

c)   E.g. What is the lowest possible score?

     E.g. How many different ways are there to score 6 on this board?

Find the right information to solve a problem...

Before you can answer a puzzle or real-life problem, you need the right information. That could mean gathering data in tables or just organising some numbers.

Write and Draw to Solve Problems

Show Your Working

EXAMPLE: Cat food comes in single tins or packs of <u>3</u>. Which is better value for money?

59p   £1.74

> You need to find the cost of <u>one tin</u> in the <u>3-pack</u>. <u>Divide</u> the <u>price</u> by the <u>number of tins</u>.

1 tin from 3-pack = £1.74 ÷ 3 = 58p

1p cheaper than the single tin.

The <u>3-pack</u> is better value for money.

Drawing a Diagram Might Help

EXAMPLE: In Clive's office block, the floors are all 10 m apart. Clive works on floor 4. He takes the lift to see his mate Burt on floor 3. Then he gets the lift to the cafe on floor 12 for coffee. Finally he gets the lift back down to his office. <u>How far has he travelled in the lift?</u>

Draw a diagram of all his journeys. He starts here, on floor 4.

> You know that each floor is 10 m above the one below.

Find the distance travelled on each leg of his journey. Then add them up to find the total distance he travelled.

$10 + 90 + 80 = \underline{180 \text{ m}}$.

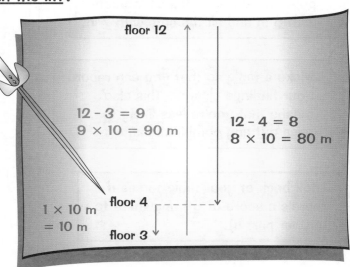

floor 12

$12 - 3 = 9$
$9 \times 10 = 90 \text{ m}$

$12 - 4 = 8$
$8 \times 10 = 80 \text{ m}$

$1 \times 10 \text{ m}$
$= 10 \text{ m}$

floor 4

floor 3

Think about Your Answer

'Real-life' problems can be tricky. Use these steps:

| <u>Read</u> the question. <u>Underline</u> the important bits. | → | Write down <u>what calculation(s)</u> you have to do. | → | <u>Estimate</u> the answer. | → | <u>Do the calculations</u>. | → | **CHECK:** Is your answer <u>sensible</u>? Are the <u>units</u> correct? |

Learning Objective:

"I can identify and record what I need to do to solve the problem, checking my answer makes sense."

Write and Draw to Solve Problems

Question 1

The picture shows the amounts of egg, tomato, mushroom and spring onion used in an omelette to feed 1 person.

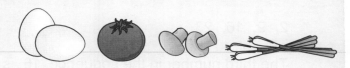

Use the information from the picture to fill in the gaps in these sentences:

a) In an omelette for 6 people, you need .... eggs, ... tomatoes and .... spring onions.

b) In an omelette with 8 eggs, you need .... tomatoes, ... mushrooms and .... spring onions. This would feed .... people.

a The amounts in the picture would feed 1 person. For 6 people, you'd need to multiply the amounts by 6.

b) **1** This time you have to work out how much you need to scale up the recipe by.

2 Multiply the amounts of all the ingredients by 4.

In an omelette for 6 people, you need 12 eggs, 6 tomatoes and 18 spring onions.

8 eggs ÷ 2 eggs = 4

In an omelette with 8 eggs, you need 4 tomatoes, 8 mushrooms and 12 spring onions.
This would feed 4 people.

Question 2

▲, ●, ◆ and ✷ each stand for a different whole number.
These equations show how they are related.

$$\blacktriangle + \blacktriangle = \bullet, \qquad 3 \times \blacklozenge = \ast, \qquad \blacktriangle + \blacklozenge = \ast, \qquad \ast + \ast = 6$$

Find the value of each symbol.

1 The best place to start with this question is to find the value of ✷.

2 Now you know ✷, you can find ◆.

3 From ✷ and ◆, you can find ▲.

4 And then find ●.

✷ + ✷ = 6, so ✷ = 3

3 × ◆ = ✷, ✷ = 3, so ◆ = 1

▲ + ◆ = ✷
✷ = 3 and ◆ = 1, so ▲ = 2

▲ + ▲ = ●, ▲ = 2, so ● = 4

Notes and diagrams can help you work stuff out...

It's not always obvious how to start solving a real-life problem or puzzle. If you get stuck, try jotting down the things you know about the problem and maybe draw a diagram.

Practice Questions

1   The rule for this sequence is 'add 7 each time'.

2, 9, 16, 23...

The third number in the sequence, 16, is a multiple of 4.
Find the next number in this sequence that is a multiple of 4.

2   Peter has five digit cards, each with a different
whole number value. The highest card has a value of 8.

If the total of the numbers on the cards is 29,
what are the values of the other 4 cards?

3   What is the value of $5n - 12$, when $n = 7$?

4   Sandy said to her friends, "*I thought of a number. When I multiplied
this number by 3 and then subtracted 6, the answer was 39.*"

Find the number that Sandy first thought of.

5   Mahliya draws a repeating pattern of stars.
The sequence of numbers continues.

a)   What colour is the 14th star in the pattern?
Choose from: black, dark blue, grey, light blue and white.

b)   Mahliya says, "The number 127 will be in a white star." Is she correct?
Explain how you know.

6   A village drama group is putting on a play of Cinderella.
Tickets cost £5 for adults and £3.50 for children.

Tom bought 14 tickets for the show and paid £64 altogether.
How many of each ticket did he buy?

Practice Questions

7 Lily and Chan carried out a survey of the trees in their local park. They wrote down the variety of each tree and made a pie chart.

a) What fraction of the trees in the park are beech trees?

b) There are 24 trees in the park. How many of them are oak trees?

c) Write down one more question you could ask about the information in the pie chart.

d) Write down one way Lily and Chan could extend their investigation.

8 The graph shows how the air temperature changed in a desert over 72 hours (3 days).

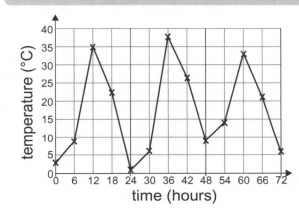

a) Estimate the highest and lowest temperatures recorded on the graph.

b) Paul says, "The temperature didn't vary as much on the third day." Explain **two** ways that the graph shows he is correct.

c) Write down one more conclusion you can draw from the graph.

9 Four school friends, Siân, Dexter, Michael and Colette, live on the same street.

Michael lives five doors down from Siân.

Colette lives eight doors up from Dexter.

Siân lives three doors up from Colette.

Where is Dexter's house on the street compared with Michael's?
Draw a diagram to help you.

10 Mrs Harte is tiling her kitchen floor. She could use either 420 small tiles or 88 large tiles. The small tiles come in packs of 30 and the large tiles come in packs of 2.

small tiles
£6.50 for 30

large tiles
£1.90 for 2

Which is the cheaper option? Show your working.

SECTION SEVEN — USING AND APPLYING MATHEMATICS

Answers

Pages 10-11 — Section One

1) a) Divide top and bottom by 5: $\dfrac{15}{10} = \dfrac{3}{2}$

   b) Divide top and bottom by 6: $\dfrac{12}{18} = \dfrac{2}{3}$

   c) Divide top and bottom by 12: $\dfrac{36}{48} = \dfrac{3}{4}$

2) a) $\dfrac{5}{2} = \dfrac{2}{2} + \dfrac{2}{2} + \dfrac{1}{2} = \mathbf{2\dfrac{1}{2}}$

   b) $\dfrac{11}{3} = \dfrac{3}{3} + \dfrac{3}{3} + \dfrac{3}{3} + \dfrac{2}{3} = \mathbf{3\dfrac{2}{3}}$

   c) $\dfrac{25}{6} = \dfrac{6}{6} + \dfrac{6}{6} + \dfrac{6}{6} + \dfrac{6}{6} + \dfrac{1}{6} = \mathbf{4\dfrac{1}{6}}$

3) $\dfrac{19}{4} = \dfrac{16}{4} + \dfrac{3}{4} = \mathbf{4\dfrac{3}{4}}$ **apples**

4) $\dfrac{5}{6} = \dfrac{10}{12}$, $\dfrac{3}{4} = \dfrac{9}{12}$ and $\dfrac{2}{3} = \dfrac{8}{12}$.

   So in order of size, the original fractions are:

   $\mathbf{\dfrac{2}{3}}$, $\mathbf{\dfrac{3}{4}}$, $\mathbf{\dfrac{5}{6}}$

   If you're struggling, then look at the FRACTIONS pages.

5)
	Percentage	Decimal	Fraction
English	85%	0.85	$\dfrac{17}{20}$
Maths	94%	0.94	$\dfrac{47}{50}$
Science	44%	0.44	$\dfrac{11}{25}$

6) –9 °C, –5 °C, –1 °C, 1 °C, 6 °C

7)
Town	Temperature at midday (°C)	Temperature at midnight (°C)	Temperature difference (°C)
Normalsville	22	4	18
Heaton	39	26	**13**
Nippiham	4	–7	**11**
Chillbeck	–6	–14	**8**

8) a) 9 to 3 (9:3), or 3 to 1 (3:1)
   b) 2 to 10 (2:10), or 1 to 5 (1:5)

   c) "8 in every 12" or $\dfrac{8}{12}$. In its simplest form

   this is "2 in every 3" or $\dfrac{2}{3}$

9) 1 in 3 = $\dfrac{1}{3}$. $\dfrac{1}{3} \times 33 = \mathbf{11}$ **ginger nuts**.

10) 2 out of every 5 is the same as $\dfrac{2}{5}$.

   $\dfrac{2}{5}$ of the total number of penguins = 8.

   So $\dfrac{1}{5}$ of the penguins = 8 ÷ 2 = 4.

   $\dfrac{3}{5}$ of the penguins do not have a black beak.

   $\dfrac{3}{5}$ of the penguins = 3 × 4 = **12 penguins**.

   If you're finding this tricky, then you need to check out PROPORTION AND RATIO.

Pages 18-19 — Section Two

1) 146 × 4 = 584
   So Ellen's answer is **right**.

2) a) No
   b) Each number in the sequence must be divisible by 5. 224 does not end in 0 or 5 so you know that 224 is not divisible by 5. This means that 224 is not in the sequence.

3) 18.2 × 11.4 ≈ 20 × 10 = **200**
   (accept 18 × 10 = 180, 18 × 11 = 198 or 20 × 11 = 220)

4) B

5) 67.51 ÷ 7.28 ≈ 70 ÷ 7 = **10**
   Estimating is one good way to check your calculations. If you need some help, have a look at the CHECKING CALCULATIONS pages.

6) 1, 2, 3, 4, 6, 9, 12, 18 and 36

7) 19, 43 and 53 are prime.

8) 48 = 2 × 24
   = 2 × 2 × 12
   = 2 × 2 × 2 × 6
   = **2 × 2 × 2 × 2 × 3**

9) 105 = 3 × 35 = **3 × 5 × 7**

10) It's less than 40 but greater than 35, so the number must be either 36, 37, 38 or 39. It is not an even number, so it can't be 36 or 38. It is a prime number, so it must be **37**.
   It's important to know your prime numbers. Take a look at the FACTORS AND MULTIPLES pages if you need some help.

11) It is a sequence of square numbers.
   64 = 8^2, so the next number must be $9^2 = \mathbf{81}$.

12) **144** ($12^2 = 144$). Other possible answers are <u>441</u> (21^2) and <u>841</u> (29^2).

13) 49 and 81 OR 9 and 121

14) a) $20^2 = 20 \times 20 = \mathbf{400}$ **marbles**.
    b) David has $30^2 = 30 \times 30 = 900$ marbles.
       So David has 900 – 400 = **500** more marbles.

Answers

Pages 34-35 — Section Three

1) a) $\frac{3}{7}$ of $1275 = \frac{3}{7} \times 1275$
$= 1275 \div 7 \times 3 = 546.42...$
So to the nearest ml, Kim used **546 ml** of lemonade.

 b) 37% of $1275 = 1275 \times \frac{37}{100}$
$= 1275 \div 100 \times 37 = 471.75$
So to the nearest ml, Kim used **472 ml** of apple juice.

2) $\frac{4}{9}$ of $1179 = 1179 \times \frac{4}{9}$
$= 1179 \div 9 \times 4 = 524$
So there are 524 mammal skulls.
This means there are
$1179 - 524 - 86 = $ **569 reptile skulls**.

3) **A**: $1000 - (160 \times 0.4)$
$= 1000 - 64 = $ **936**
B: $975 \div (50 + 490)$
$= 975 \div 540 = $ **1.80555...**
C: $(1000 - 160) \times 0.4$
$= 840 \times 0.4 = $ **336**
D: $(975 \div 50) + 490$
$= 19.5 + 490 = $ **509.5**

4) a) $\sqrt{63} = 7.94$ (to 2 decimal places)

 b) $\sqrt{197} = 14.04$ (to 2 decimal places)
 Look at the pages on CALCULATORS if you made any mistakes with these questions.

5) a) $56 \div 100 = $ **0.56**
 b) $1000 \times 0.21 = $ **210**
 c) $10 \times $ **0.05** $= 0.5$
 d) $45 \div $ **1000** $= 0.045$

6) a) In total, Louise spends:

```
   8.75
  19.59
+  0.61
  28.95
  1 1 1
```

 She pays with two £20 notes, which is £40.

```
 3 9 9 1
 4̶0̶.0̶0̶
-28.95
 11.05
```

 Louise gets **£11.05** change.

 b)
```
   8 1
 28.9̶5
-15.89
 13.06
```

 Ben spends **£13.06** less than Louise.

7) Olivia has been alive for 1 leap year plus 6 normal years.
 Find the number of days in six normal years:

```
  365
×   6
 2190
 3 3
```

 Add on the number of days in a leap year:

```
 2190
+ 366
 2556
    1
```

 Olivia has been alive for **2556 days**.

8) a) Divide 316 by 4.

```
   079
4 )31̄1̄6
```

 There are **79 children** in each team.

 b) Cost of the children's tickets:

```
  316
×   3
  948
    1
```

 Cost of the teachers' tickets = 9 × £5 = £45
 Add these together:

```
  948
+  45
  993
    1
```

 So the overall cost is **£993**.

9) a)
```
          288
        × 43
288 × 3→  864
288 × 40→11520
        12384
```

 So Paul got **£12 384** that year.

 b)
```
      0 2 4
12 )2²8 8
   -2 4 0
      4 8
```

 Paul spends **£24** on bacon.

10) a) The cost of the mince is £2.58 × 8.
 Work out 258 × 8 first, then divide by 100.

```
  258
×   8
 2064
```

 $2064 \div 100 = 20.64$.
 Now subtract £20.64 from £25:

```
 2⁴5̶.⁹0̶¹0̶
-20.64
  4.36
```

 The teacher gets **£4.36** change.

Answers

b) 2.58 kg = 2.58 × 1000 g = 2580 g.
Divide 2580 by 6:

$$\begin{array}{r} 0430 \\ 6\overline{)2580} \end{array}$$

So each child gets **430 grams** of mince.
Multiplying and dividing can be tough. If you found this question hard, take a look at the pages on WRITTEN MULTIPLYING AND DIVIDING.

Pages 46-47 — Section Four

1) a) 180° is a straight line, so 190° is just a little bit more than a straight line.
So **Angle C** is approximately 190°.

b) An acute angle is less than 90°.
Angle A is an acute angle.

2) Angle A = 117°
Angle B = 31°

3) Angle z = 180° – 63° – 63° = **54°**

4) Angle X = 360° ÷ 8 = **45°**

5) Point C is horizontally level with coordinate (1, 2) — so they must have the same y-coordinate. It's 2. The kite is symmetrical.
So the horizontal distance between point C and (–1, 4) is the same as the horizontal distance between (1, 2) and (–1, 4).
Look at the x-coordinates.
1 is two units to the right of –1.
So the x-coordinate of C must be –1 – 2 = –3.
So C has coordinates **(–3, 2)**.
Negative coordinates, hmmm. Just take a deep breath and see what you need to do. It's often a bit easier than it looks.
If you need some help, have a look at the COORDINATES pages.

6) a) None (there are no mirror lines)

b) 2

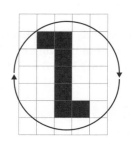

7) a) and b)

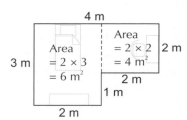

8) The shape has been translated 3 squares to the left and 3 squares up.

9)

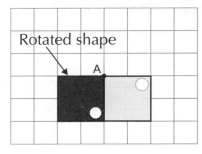
Rotated shape
A

If you need some help with this question, take a look at the TRANSFORMATIONS pages.

Pages 56-57 — Section Five

1) The perimeter of Arthur's field
= 20 + 15 + 20 + 15 = 70 metres.
So Arthur **will not** have enough fencing.

2) a) Perimeter of classroom
= 8 + 6 + 8 + 6 = **28 m**

b) Area of classroom = 8 × 6 = **48 m²**

3) a) There are two missing lengths.
These are: 3 – 2 = 1 m,
    and   4 – 2 = 2 m.
So perimeter of bedroom
= 4 + 2 + 2 + 1 + 2 + 3 = **14 m**

b) Divide the bedroom into smaller shapes.

```
              4 m
    ┌──────┬────────┐
    │      │  Area  │ 2 m
3 m │ Area │ = 2 × 2│
    │=2 × 3│ = 4 m² │
    │= 6 m²│  2 m   │
    │      └────────┘
    │          1 m
    └──────┘
      2 m
```

Total area = 6 + 4 = **10 m²**

4) Area of garden = 4 × 5 = 20 m²
Area of pond = 2 × 3 = 6 m²
So the area of the garden, not including the pond, is 20 – 6 = **14 m²**

5) Area of smaller piece of material
= 6 × 7 = 42 m²
Area of larger piece of material
= 9 × 8 = 72 m²
So the total area of the material
= 42 + 72 = **114 m²**
If these seem hard, then take a look at the pages on CALCULATING PERIMETER AND AREA.

6) a) A normal bucket holds **about 10 litres** (but any answer between 5 litres and 20 litres is acceptable).

b) An average egg has a mass of **about 50 grams** (but any answer between 20 grams and 200 grams is acceptable).

Answers

c) An average car has a length of **about 3 metres** (but any answer between 2 metres and 4 metres is acceptable).

7) Mass of the 25 chocolates without the box
= 100 g – 25 g = 75 grams.
So the mass of one chocolate
= 75 g ÷ 25 = **3 grams**

8) Convert the masses in kilograms to grams.
2 kg = 2 × 1000 g = 2000 g
2.4 kg = 2.4 × 1000 g = 2400 g
So the five masses (in grams) in order are:
2 g, 20 g, 2000 g, 2400 g, 2500 g.
Now write these masses as they were written in the question. This means the order is:
2 g, 20 g, 2 kg, 2.4 kg, 2500 g.

9) Convert Alice's 5.6 km to metres:
5.6 km = 5.6 × 1000 m = 5600 m
This is further than Paul's 5100 m,
so **Alice cycled further**.

10) There are 10 divisions between each numbered mark. The difference between each numbered mark = 1 kg. So each division is worth 1 kg ÷ 10 = 0.1 kg.
Donald already has 1.2 kg, so he needs a further 2 – 1.2 = 0.8 kg.
In grams this is 0.8 × 1000 g = **800 grams**

11) Convert Anne's height to cm.
1.31 m = 1.31 × 100 cm = 131 cm.
So Anne is 131 – 126 = **5 cm** taller than Beth.

12)a) 3.5 m = 3 × 100 cm + 50 cm = **350 cm**
b) 1 metre ≈ 3 feet, 0.5 metre ≈ 1.5 feet
so 3.5 metres ≈ 3 × 3 + 1.5 feet = **10.5 feet**

13) 8 kilometres ≈ 5 miles
72 ÷ 8 = 9, so 9 × 5 miles = **45 miles**
If you need help with this, take a look at the pages on UNITS AND MEASURES.

Pages 68-69 — Section Six

1) a) The probability of spinning a 2 on the square spinner is $\frac{1}{4}$.
The probability of spinning a 2 on the 8-sided spinner is $\frac{2}{8} = \frac{1}{4}$.
So the chance of spinning a 2 is the same for both spinners.

b) The probability of spinning an odd number on the square spinner is $\frac{2}{4} = \frac{1}{2}$.
The probability of spinning an odd number on the 8-sided spinner is $\frac{2}{8} = \frac{1}{4}$.
This means the chance of spinning an odd number is different for the two spinners.

2) There are 12 – 3 – 1 = 8 green counters.
So the probability of picking a green counter is $\frac{8}{12} = \frac{2}{3}$.

3) a) In order, the marks are:
8, 9, 12, 12, 13, 15, 16, 18, 19, 20
The mode (the most common mark) is **12**.

b) The middle position is halfway between 13 and 15, so the median is **14**.

4) E.g. **5, 6, 7**
5 + 6 + 7 = 18. 18 ÷ 3 = 6.
(There are loads of other answers you could have.)

5) a) The range of Bob's times is
34.1 – 30.2 = 3.9 seconds
The range of Dave's times is
35.0 – 30.1 = 4.9 seconds
So **Dave's** times have the greater range.

b) Bob's mean $= \dfrac{30.2 + 32.1 + 34.1 + 31.2 + 34.0}{5}$
$= \dfrac{161.6}{5} = 32.32$ s

Dave's mean $= \dfrac{30.1 + 31.5 + 33.6 + 35.0 + 30.5}{5}$
$= \dfrac{160.7}{5} = 32.14$ s

Dave has the faster mean time, so **Dave wins**.

6) The total of the distances is 11.7 m.
So the mean distance is 11.7 ÷ 10 = **1.17 m**
*This type of question can be a bit tricky.
If you need some help, check out the
ANALYSING DATA pages.*

7) a) 9 – 4.5 = **4.5 hours**
b) In week 1, the hours were:
7.5, 9, 3, 4, 8, 6, 5.5
In order, these are: 3, 4, 5.5, 6, 7.5, 8, 9
The median (middle value) = **6 hours**

8) The angle for "tennis" is 30°.
As a fraction of the whole pie chart, this is
$\frac{30}{360} = \frac{1}{12}$.
The whole pie chart shows 72 people, so the number that chose tennis must be
$\frac{1}{12} \times 72 = 72 \div 12 = $ **6 people**.

9) a) 120
b) The number of jumpers sold increases after August, probably because the weather is turning colder as winter approaches.
Look back at the TABLES AND CHARTS pages for more practice with this kind of thing.

Answers

Pages 76-77 — Section Seven

1) The next numbers in the sequence are
30, 37, 44... **44** is a multiple of 4.
Read the pages on NUMBER PATTERNS if you made a mistake here.

2) The total of the 4 cards should be 29 − 8 = 21.
All four cards must have a different number less than 8 on, so try the numbers 7, 6, 5 and 4. This gives a total of 4 + 5 + 6 + 7 = 22. This is one too many... and the only number that you can reduce by one is the '4' (otherwise the numbers won't all be different). So the other values must be **3, 5, 6** and **7**.

3) $5 \times 7 − 12 = 35 − 12 = $ **23**

4) Use ▲ for the unknown number.
First, you need to add 6 to 39 — this will tell you what "3 times ▲" is, or 3▲.
3▲ = 39 + 6 = 45
Now divide 45 by 3 to find ▲.
▲ = 45 ÷ 3 = 15
So the number Sandy thought of was **15**.

5) a) There are 5 colours in the sequence which repeat.
So the 5th and 10th stars are white, and then the sequence starts again. This means that the 14th star will be the fourth colour in the sequence — **light blue**.
b) Mahliya is **wrong**.
The white stars will be in positions 5, 10, 15, 20, 25 etc which are all multiples of 5. Since 127 is not a multiple of 5, it will not be a white star.

6) You could draw a table to show what different combinations of adult and child tickets cost.

Number of adult tickets	Number of child tickets	Total cost (£)
14	0	14 × 5 = **70**
13	1	13 × 5 + 1 × 3.5 = **68.5**
12	2	12 × 5 + 2 × 3.5 = **67**
11	3	11 × 5 + 3 × 3.5 = **65.5**
10	4	10 × 5 + 4 × 3.5 = **64**
9	5	

You can stop your table here. You can see that **Tom bought 10 adult tickets and 4 child tickets**.

7) a) The circle is divided into 12 sections, and beech takes up 4 of these sections. So the fraction of beech trees in the park is
$\frac{4}{12}$, or $\frac{1}{3}$.
b) One quarter of all the sections in the pie chart are taken up by oak trees. So the number of oak trees in the park is $\frac{1}{4} \times 24 = 24 \div 4 = $ **6**.
c) E.g. How many willow trees are in the park? What fraction of the trees are ash?

d) E.g. They could investigate the trees in other parks in their area.
They could investigate which trees are the biggest/smallest.

8) a) Highest: approximately 38 °C
Lowest: approximately 1 °C
b) Paul is correct because:
1) the highest temperature on the third day is not as high as the highest temperature on the other two days, and...
2) the lowest temperature on the third day is not as low as the lowest temperature on the other two days.
c) E.g. The temperature varied most on the second day.
The temperature rose for 12 hours each day and then fell for 12 hours each day.

9) Draw a 'map' of the houses, and mark on the first two pieces of information you know — don't worry about the third piece of information for now.

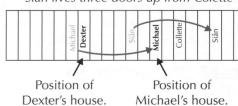

Now move <u>both</u> Siân <u>and</u> Michael so that...
Siân lives three doors up from Colette

So Dexter lives six doors down from Michael.

For more help, check out the WRITE AND DRAW TO SOLVE PROBLEMS pages.

10) Using small tiles:
She would need 420 ÷ 30 = 14 packs of small tiles. This would cost 14 × £6.50 = **£91**.
Using large tiles:
She would need 88 ÷ 2 = 44 packs of large tiles. This would cost 44 × £1.90 = **£83.60**.
So using large tiles would be cheaper.

Index

Index